ISBN 978-1-331-42932-6
PIBN 10188977

This book is a reproduction of an important historical work. Forgotten Books uses
state-of-the-art technology to digitally reconstruct the work, preserving the original format
whilst repairing imperfections present in the aged copy. In rare cases, an imperfection in
the original, such as a blemish or missing page, may be replicated in our edition. We do,
however, repair the vast majority of imperfections successfully; any imperfections that
remain are intentionally left to preserve the state of such historical works.

1 MONTH OF
FREE
READING

at
www.ForgottenBooks.com

By purchasing this book you are eligible for one month membership to ForgottenBooks.com, giving you unlimited access to our entire collection of over 1,000,000 titles via our web site and mobile apps.

To claim your free month visit:

www.forgottenbooks.com/free188977

English
Français
Deutsche
Italiano
Español
Português

www.forgottenbooks.com

Mythology Photography **Fiction**
Fishing Christianity **Art** Cooking
Essays Buddhism Freemasonry
Medicine **Biology** Music **Ancient
Egypt** Evolution Carpentry Physics
Dance Geology **Mathematics** Fitness
Shakespeare **Folklore** Yoga Marketing
Confidence Immortality Biographies
Poetry **Psychology** Witchcraft
Electronics Chemistry History **Law**
Accounting **Philosophy** Anthropology
Alchemy Drama Quantum Mechanics
Atheism Sexual Health **Ancient History**
Entrepreneurship Languages Sport
Paleontology Needlework Islam
Metaphysics Investment Archaeology
Parenting Statistics Criminology
Motivational

HEARINGS

BEFORE THE

COMMITTEE ON AGRICULTURE AND FORESTRY

OF THE

UNITED STATES SENATE

ON THE BILL

(H. R. 18537) MAKING APPROPRIATIONS FOR THE DEPARTMENT OF AGRICUL-TURE FOR THE FISCAL YEAR ENDING JUNE 30, 1907.

FIFTY-NINTH CONGRESS, FIRST SESSION.

WASHINGTON:
GOVERNMENT PRINTING OFFICE.
1906.

AGRICULTURE APPROPRIATION BILL.

COMMITTEE ON AGRICULTURE AND FORESTRY,
UNITED STATES SENATE,
Washington, D. C., Monday, May 7, 1906.

The committee met at 11 o'clock a. m.

Present: Senators Proctor (chairman), Hansbrough, Warren, Burnham, Perkins, Long, Money, Simmons, Frazier, and Latimer.

Present, also, Hon. James Wilson, Secretary of Agriculture, and Dr. B. T. Galloway, Chief of the Bureau of Plant Industry, Department of Agriculture.

The committee thereupon proceeded to the consideration of the bill (H. R. 18537) "Making appropriations for the Department of Agriculture for the fiscal year ending June 30, 1907."

STATEMENT OF HON. JAMES WILSON, SECRETARY OF AGRICULTURE.

The CHAIRMAN. Mr. Secretary, I would be glad to have you tell us in a general way what points you wish to be heard on, and what bureaus, especially, you wish to have represented here by their chiefs; the general scope of your wishes, and then any particular points that you can bring to our attention to-day.

Secretary WILSON. Heretofore, Mr. Chairman, if you will remember, you have read the bill over while I was here, and when points I had to make came up I called your attention to them while the bill was being read over. Then you considered it in executive session afterwards. I do not think it is necessary to bring the chiefs up here. Doctor Galloway has always done a great deal in the way of assisting in getting up the bill, and he knows more about it than any of the other chiefs; so I have brought him to help along that line.

The bill has gone through the House. I was not present in the committee when it was under consideration. They send for the chiefs in the House committee and have full hearings.

The CHAIRMAN. They sent for all the chiefs?

Secretary WILSON. They sent for all the chiefs, but they did not send for me.

Senator HANSBROUGH. And their hearings have been printed, and we have them.

Secretary WILSON. Yes; except on one or two points that they wanted to hear me about.

The CHAIRMAN. You were before them, were you?

Secretary WILSON. I was before them regarding one or two points, that was all; but the bill generally I did not say anything about.

Now, I have made estimates, and I would like to have my estimates brought to your attention here. To some of them the House has paid no attention, to some of them it has, and consequently I would like to present the estimates just as I made them all the way through. You have here in this bill what the House did. I want to ask you to consider the estimates in connection with what the House did.

Senator SIMMONS. Mr. Secretary, how would it do for us to take the bill up by sections, and when we reach each section, without reading it, for you to let us know whether you have any suggestions to make about that section?

Secretary WILSON. That is the way you have always done, and I think you can go through the bill very rapidly in that way. Of course the bill deals with the whole Department, and there are a great many things to be said about the whole bill; but there is a great deal of it where there are no amendments. Some of the bureaus scarcely have a change.

The CHAIRMAN. Taking up the bill, then, the first thing you ask for is to have the salary of your solicitor raised to $3,000.

Secretary WILSON. That is the first thing. I think that solicitor should have $3,000.

The CHAIRMAN. What particular reasons can you give for the increase?

Secretary WILSON. As the Department grows and as we are interested in doing a great many different things—building, and making contracts with experiment stations for cooperative work, for supplies, and all that—we find it necessary to have men of good legal attainments to see to it that we do not go wrong, and I do not think $3,000 is out of the way for a man of that caliber.

Senator HANSBROUGH. You have a very good man in Mr. McCabe.

Secretary WILSON. Yes; we have a very good man.

The CHAIRMAN. How does this salary compare with the salaries of others in other Departments doing similar work?

Secretary WILSON. I think they generally get about $4,500.

Senator MONEY. Mr. Secretary, is there an assistant attorney-general for your Department?

Secretary WILSON. No; we have what they call a solicitor down there.

Senator MONEY. He is not called an assistant attorney-general?

Secretary WILSON. No; he is not an assistant attorney-general at all.

The CHAIRMAN. He is not in that class at all; he is paid $2,500.

Senator MONEY. And he is called a solicitor?

Secretary WILSON. Yes.

The CHAIRMAN. He is paid $2,500, which would put him in the class of assistant attorneys in the Attorney-General's office—not an assistant attorney-general, you know, but assistant attorneys, that are paid from $2,000 or $2,200 up to $3,000. Three thousand dollars is a common salary for assistant attorneys there.

Senator MONEY. Are you sure of that, Mr. Chairman?

The CHAIRMAN. One man, Mr. Button, who was clerk of this committee for a time since I have been chairman, was an assistant attorney for several years, with a salary of $3,000; and it is my impression that the duties of those assistants attorneys were not so important, even, as the duties of this solicitor, because they never had to act independently. They were assigned certain duties, to collect evidence in certain cases, and prepare them for trial.

Senator MONEY. Does Mr. McCabe ever have to go into court at all?

Doctor GALLOWAY. Yes, sir.

Senator MONEY. He has to go into court?

Doctor GALLOWAY. Yes, sir.

Senator MONEY. In what kinds of cases, Doctor?

Doctor GALLOWAY. Different cases that come before the Department involving legal work. For example, if we have a case in the Department of Justice in reference to a claim for damages in the matter of one of our new buildings, Mr. McCabe assists the attorneys in the Department of Justice. If a party in Texas, who has had certain cattle condemned and destroyed, files in the Court of Claims a suit for damages, our solicitor must help the attorney in the Court of Claims defend the Department's case.

Senator MONEY. Is that all he does, then—assist the Department of Justice?

Doctor GALLOWAY. No, sir; he prepares all legal documents in connection with the Department's work—all of our contracts for buildings, and all other contracts. He prepares all of our patent cases, where we have to file patents to protect the Government against private monopoly on matters that may be discovered in the Department. In fact, he attends to all the legal work of the Department.

Senator MONEY. He is a sort of a law clerk?

Doctor GALLOWAY. A sort of a law clerk; yes, sir.

Senator MONEY. As a matter of fact, then, it is not absolutely necessary for him to assist the Department of Justice at the trial?

Doctor GALLOWAY. No, sir; but our experience has been that those men can never get the full details of the cases as one of our own men can, so that we always have Mr. McCabe or the man who holds this position as an assistant.

Senator HANSBROUGH. He has no assistant, then?

Doctor GALLOWAY. None except a few clerks.

The CHAIRMAN. Senator Money, this Department, you know, is doing business in every State of the Union, and oftentimes the local laws have to be looked up.

Senator MONEY. Yes; I see the necessity for his being there, but I wanted to know exactly what his duties were. If he has to go into court, I think we had better leave that to the Department of Justice; but if it is a matter confined to the Department—a matter of contract, as you remark, where the statutes are different—we ought to have a man who is familiar with them, or who knows how to look them up, at least, which the ordinary layman can not do.

Senator BURNHAM. His time is pretty well taken up?

Doctor GALLOWAY. Yes; he is behind nearly always, he has so many things to attend to.

Senator MONEY. He confines himself exclusively, then, to your work, does he?

Doctor GALLOWAY. Yes, sir.

Senator MONEY. He does not do anything else but that. He ought to be a pretty fair lawyer, then.

Secretary WILSON. I think he is, along those lines.

The CHAIRMAN. The next point, Mr. Secretary, where you make an increase, is in line 13, page 2, where you ask for two inspectors.

Secretary WILSON. We have in the Department a very great many inspectors. We have several hundred of them in the Bureau of Animal Industry, etc., and we have them in the several Bureaus. But I would like to have two inspectors who shall report directly to me, that I can send confidentially to look after a piece of work that is being done or a class of men doing work anywhere, and have them report confidentially to me what that condition of affairs is.

You will remember that a year ago last June we had one of our trusted men in the Bureau of Statistics give confidential reports to New York gamblers. On that occasion I felt at a great loss as to what to do in this line. I went to the Treasury Department and got their secret-service men; but I felt greatly handicapped. I want some competent person to take hold of a thing of that kind and go to the bottom of it, and look it all up.

We have charges now against the integrity of our work in the inspection of meats, etc. We have 155 abattoirs where meats are cured, and we have people there everywhere; the Government money is being spent very extensively. We would like to have somebody, not known to them, to drop in there and see what they are doing, similar to the inspectors the Post-Office Department has, who report to the Secretary. They have a whole host of inspectors, and I thought I would like to have two. The House has refused to give them.

The CHAIRMAN. You might call them, perhaps, " general inspectors; " would you?

Secretary WILSON. Yes; something of that kind. They might be called anything along that line. I want them really to see how the Government moneys are being expended everywhere. We are working in every part of the United States.

Senator HANSBROUGH. Some of the other Departments have inspectors such as you want here?

Secretary WILSON. I think so.

Senator BURNHAM. You have not any officials who are in a position to perform that duty?

Secretary WILSON. I can generally pick up a man, and take him away from his work, whatever it is; but those men are not trained in doing that kind of thing. That is the trouble. It requires men who are peculiarly constituted.

Senator MONEY. How much do you want to pay them?

Secretary WILSON. Oh, we can get them for $2,000; then it will take $2,000 more, perhaps, to pay their expenses. It might cost around that sum.

Senator MONEY. Mr. Chairman, I think that is a good suggestion. I think it would save a good deal more than it costs, and it would be a great satisfaction to the Secretary to know that he is not imposed upon.

The CHAIRMAN. We will go on, then, to the clerks in line 16. You ask for two more of class 1.

Secretary WILSON. These are the clerks for the solicitor; that is what they are.

Senator BURNHAM. You have an estimate of " eight clerks of class 1, $7,200." You would increase the amount, I suppose?

Secretary WILSON. No; this just gives us the authority.

The CHAIRMAN. You want two more clerks——

Doctor GALLOWAY. Two more clerks of class 1; we ask to have it read " eight " instead of " six," in line 16.

Senator MONEY. What are they to do?

Doctor GALLOWAY. They are to assist the solicitor in his office work.

Senator MONEY. Oh, they are law clerks?

Doctor GALLOWAY. No; they are not law clerks; they are ordinary clerks that are wanted to prepare the documents and contracts and all the different papers, etc.

Secretary WILSON. To do stenographic work.

Doctor GALLOWAY. To do stenographic work and that kind of work.

Secretary WILSON. They are not law clerks.

The CHAIRMAN. I was thinking, Doctor Galloway, that you spoke about a clerk of class 2.

Doctor GALLOWAY. Yes, sir; one extra clerk of class 2. That would be in line 15; instead of " two " there it would be " three."

The CHAIRMAN. And in that case would you not reduce the clerks of class 1 to seven instead of eight?

Doctor GALLOWAY. That can be done; yes, sir.

Senator MONEY. Doctor Galloway, what did the House give in addition to what you had before? Did it give you anything at all in the way of additional——

Doctor GALLOWAY. Additional appropriation for the whole Department?

Senator MONEY. Yes.

Doctor GALLOWAY. Oh, yes; we got something.

Secretary WILSON. We got an increase of $400,000 in the House.

Senator MONEY. I mean in the clerical force?

Doctor GALLOWAY. Very little in that line—scarcely anything.

Senator MONEY. Mr. Chairman, excuse me, but I would like to ask a question right here, for fear I may forget it. It is not in this bill, of course, but relates to a general legislative condition. I would like to know the number of persons on what you call the laborers' roll, but men who really do clerical work in your Department. About how many are there?

Secretary WILSON. Those who have been in suspense with regard to the way they got into the Department, and the way they were covered in, etc., have been required to take a civil-service examination before we could promote them; consequently they appear as laborers on the rolls, but they do clerical work. There are not so many of them now.

Senator MONEY. But they could be admitted to the clerical roll by standing the examination, could they, if they chose to do so?

Secretary WILSON. Oh, yes, sir.

Doctor GALLOWAY. A great many of them are doing that.

Senator FRAZIER. They have to be in the Department two years first, do they not?

Secretary WILSON. Most of them have been in the Department five or six or eight years.

Senator FRAZIER. But the rule requires that they shall be in for two years before they can stand the examination, does it not?

Secretary WILSON. Yes; but that rule does not cover them. The order that covers there is one from the President, requiring them to go through the civil-service examination before we promote them. They are gradually working through.

Senator MONEY. That is what I wanted to know.

Doctor GALLOWAY. About fifty of them went through last year.

Senator MONEY. I was thinking about the scientific aids.

Doctor GALLOWAY. That has been eliminated by the Civil Service Commission. We have no scientific aids now.

Senator MONEY. How do you get hold of them?

Doctor GALLOWAY. How do we get hold of these young men?

Senator MONEY. Yes.

Doctor GALLOWAY. By minor examinations. We have changed the name of the thing, but we have practically the same sort of an examination to bring in minor grades.

Senator MONEY. But you still have that force?

Doctor GALLOWAY. Oh, yes; we get the bulk of our people from our agricultural colleges.

Senator MONEY. There is no lack of them here?

Doctor GALLOWAY. No.

Secretary WILSON. We do not have them on probation, as we used to; we get them direct by examination when they are competent to take it.

Doctor GALLOWAY. The Commission objected to the filing of papers showing evidence of graduation.

Senator MONEY. And those theses required by the Department of the college graduates—they objected to that?

Doctor GALLOWAY. They did not object to the principle, but they wanted a specific examination to cover all the points. They objected to the theses part and to the graduation part on the ground that it did not give a basis for comparison. That is, one college in one State would give a very different course of training from a college in another State, so that they wanted an examination that would give an equal basis of standing for the whole country. We agreed on that, and we are getting our young men in in that way now.

Senator BURNHAM. Let me ask this question, Mr. Secretary: On what basis are these persons paid who are on the rolls as laborers and who are performing the work of clerks?

Secretary WILSON. About the highest pay you can give a laborer.

Senator BURNHAM. But it is laborers' pay?

Secretary WILSON. Yes.

Senator MONEY. What is the highest?

Doctor GALLOWAY. Sixty dollars a month.

Senator MONEY. Can you not give them seventy?

Doctor GALLOWAY. No, sir.

Senator MONEY. You can not give more than sixty?

Secretary WILSON. No, sir; $60 a month is as high as we can go for a laborer. Then, when they take the examination and get through we can increase their pay, and we do.

Senator MONEY. Is that provision that you can not give them higher than $60 a law or a regulation?

Secretary WILSON. It is a regulation; but it binds us just about as strongly, you know.

Senator MONEY. I know that; but sometimes a department has a way of supplementing the legislation of Congress by regulations which are not exactly in accordance with it. I can recollect when I was under the painful necessity of having a writ of mandamus issued on the Postmaster-General to make him obey the law, and to avoid it he got the law changed.

The CHAIRMAN. Senator Money, in the very last clause of the last bill, which the clerk will show you, the House put on a provision in regard to the clerks that had been laborers and had been taken in by the President's order. They were taken into the civil service. There was quite a long debate in the Senate about the matter, and it was plainly the purpose of the Senate, as I think you will see by looking at that debate, that those persons thus taken in should be in the civil service in full, and subject like all others in the civil service to promotion without examination.

Senator MONEY. I recollect that.

The CHAIRMAN. But the Civil Service Commission wanted the matter to go through their hands, and I suppose at their request the President issued an order that before promotion they should pass a civil-service examination, and that has been in force since. In the discussion in the Senate, in which Senator Allison, Senator Hale, and a good many of the Senators took part, the ground was taken that satisfactory service for several years was certainly equivalent to, if not better, than any examination.

Senator MONEY. A thousand times better.

The CHAIRMAN. But the Civil Service Commission thought the examination was necessary and got an order to that effect. That is the way the matter stands.

Senator MONEY. I recollect that; that is the reason I asked these questions. I do not like to have the President of an autocratic Civil Service Commission step in with an order to do what I consider contradicts the plain meaning of Congress in the matter.

The CHAIRMAN. That would very naturally come up the very last thing in the bill, as it was the last paragraph of the last bill.

Senator BURNHAM. I suppose we could legislate so as to have our legislation control in a matter of that kind, could we not?

Senator MONEY. Why, yes; all we have to do is to say, in a few words here, that the Secretary shall promote as he chooses, in his discretion.

The CHAIRMAN. We will consider that subject later. Mr. Secretary, you ask for these additional clerks for what reason? That the business of your office has increased?

Secretary WILSON. Yes; and that the solicitor has so much more work to do that I have had to give him a stenographer and typewriter to help him. That is what these two clerks are—stenographers and typewriters to the solicitor.

The CHAIRMAN. The next changes, I believe, are merely of figures.

Secretary WILSON. The next item is, " One fireman, who shall be a steam fitter, $1,000," instead of " $900."

Doctor GALLOWAY. You give him $100 more?

Secretary WILSON. We give him $100 more. He is a very excellent man and has been there a long time, and it is a moderate salary. It is not quite as much as they get outside.

The CHAIRMAN. And you ask for an increase in the salary of the painter?

Secretary WILSON. We ask for an increase of $100 for a painter.

The CHAIRMAN. The wages of those men in outside service are steadily increasing, I suppose?

Secretary WILSON. Oh, yes; but we have not increased ours very much, and ours do not get as much as they do outside, because our employment is steady.

Doctor GALLOWAY. This man in line 23, the $900 man, has been getting that $900 for a number of years.

The CHAIRMAN. The next item is on page 3, at the bottom of the page.

Secretary WILSON. There is a painter there at $840 instead of $720, as proposed.

The CHAIRMAN. For the same reasons you gave before?

Secretary WILSON. The same reasons; yes.

Senator HANSBROUGH. Did you ask for all of these things in the House?

Secretary WILSON. Oh, yes; we asked for them in the House. What they gave us in the House is not shown in this bill, you know.

Senator HANSBROUGH. No.

Secretary WILSON. I think they gave very little along that line in the House, Senator.

The CHAIRMAN. All increases are shown on the bill.

Doctor GALLOWAY. Yes; the increases are shown.

The CHAIRMAN. They are shown by being in italics.

Doctor GALLOWAY. This is the House bill just as it passed, and the House amendments are in italics.

Senator FRAZIER. Are the increases that were made in the House indicated in this bill?

The CHAIRMAN. All changes from the last appropriation bill are indicated by italics.

Senator HANSBROUGH. All House changes.

Senator FRAZIER. Then the item that the Secretary last referred to, at the bottom of page 3, was increased in the House. That seems to be in italics—$720. The House raised it to $720, and now they ask for $840.

The CHAIRMAN. Now, on page 4——

Doctor GALLOWAY. Those are just changes in the footings.

The CHAIRMAN. On page 4, line 6, there seems to be a reduction of rent.

Senator FRAZIER. I suppose there will be no objection to that.

Doctor GALLOWAY. That simply comes out of the Secretary's lump fund for the payment of rents. He finds that the $7,600 is enough, and the rest can be used for miscellaneous expenses connected with the general service. The Secretary has what we call a lump fund here of $10,000 for paying rents and other expenses, and he finds that $7,600 will be sufficient; and the rest of the funds can therefore be used for other miscellaneous expenses connected with his office, including the salaries of two clerks for the solicitor, which are transferred to the statutory roll.

Senator SIMMONS. How would you get the rest unless it is included in the appropriation? You are simply decreasing the appropriation here.

Doctor GALLOWAY. It does not decrease the appropriation, Senator; it simply decreases the mandatory requirement on the Secretary to pay $10,000 for rent.

Senator SIMMONS. I see.

The CHAIRMAN. I see nothing else marked until we get to page 8.

Senator FRAZIER. There is a change in line 16, on page 4.

Senator BURNHAM. Lines 16 and 21 and 22.

Doctor GALLOWAY. We have nothing that the Secretary asks for there.

Senator MONEY. There is nothing marked in the copy I have here.

Senator BURNHAM. In my copy of the bill at line 16 it says: "One chief of supplies, at $1,800, omitted." What does that mean, Doctor?

Doctor GALLOWAY. We did not put that in. I do not know anything about that.

Senator HANSBROUGH. Mr. Chairman, as I understand, we are to hear the Secretary on those things to which he desires to call the attention of the committee—the increases and changes over the bill as it passed the House.

Doctor GALLOWAY. The only change in the Weather Bureau items are the mere verbal ones. On page 8 there is one change, in line 7; and on the same page, in line 11, there is another change. They are merely verbal changes. Those are the only changes that the Secretary wishes made in the Weather Bureau.

Senator MONEY. At what sum did the House fix Doctor Moore's salary?

Doctor GALLOWAY. They did not change it.

Senator MONEY. He wants a thousand dollars more, does he not? What does the Secretary want? How about that, Mr. Secretary, if you please?

Secretary WILSON. You refer to increasing the salary of the Chief of the Weather Bureau?

Senator MONEY. Yes; one or two members of the House came over and asked me if I would not propose an increase of $1,000 in the salary of Mr. Moore, the Chief of the Weather Bureau. I do not know what he is getting. He is getting $5,000 now, is he not?

Doctor GALLOWAY. He is getting $5,000 now; yes.

Senator MONEY. They have allowed him a horse and buggy, and he does not want that, I believe; but he would like to have $1,000 more in salary.

Secretary WILSON. I have not made any estimate for any increase there. It came to my attention two days ago that the House proposed to give him the use of a horse and carriage, owing to the fact that he is located at a considerable distance from the main Department. Then the proposition has been made that he would rather have so much money than to have that, and buy his own horses. That is the proposition as I have heard it. I do not want to take the position that Mr. Moore is not worth $6,000 to the Government; I think he is.

Senator WARREN. Mr. Secretary, Doctor Moore sometimes serves as Assistant Secretary, does he not?

Secretary WILSON. Yes, sir; he sometimes serves as Assistant Secretary.

Senator WARREN. He is rather isolated in his office?

Secretary WILSON. Yes; he is isolated. He probably needs a horse more than any other chief needs one, unless it might be the Forester.

Senator WARREN. I think that whatever we do about that it had better be in the way of an increase in salary rather than giving him a horse. He has probably gone into the horse business already, and gotten his horses and his wagons, and if we give him an official carriage which his family can not use, it will put him in a worse condition in some ways than otherwise. If he has his team, and all that, I think it would be better to pay him more and let him furnish his own horse, and then he can use it for his private personal use and be independent.

Secretary WILSON. I do not think I would advise the committee to disturb that law with regard to horses and carriages.

Senator WARREN. It debars their use, you know.   .

Secretary WILSON. It debars their use. I think that was a good law. Just let it stay so. .

Senator MONEY. And not have any public carriages?

Secretary WILSON. I think not.

Senator MONEY. I think it was a great abuse.

Senator WARREN. Now, Mr. Secretary, let me ask you this question: We raised the salary of this position $500 some years ago. What was the original salary? How long was the salary at that figure?

Doctor GALLOWAY. Professor Moore's salary has been $5,000 for, I think, eight or nine years.

Senator WARREN. I was thinking it was seven. Before that it was how much?   .

Doctor GALLOWAY. Four thousand five hundred dollars.

Senator WARREN. Now, how far back does the inauguration of that salary date before his time?

Doctor GALLOWAY. It dates back to the time when the Bureau was in the War Department.

Senator WARREN. Twenty years ago, or such a matter?

Doctor GALLOWAY. Yes, sir.

Senator WARREN. Then it was always $4,500, was it, from its inception up to the time that we raised Professor Moore's salary $500?

.· Doctor GALLOWAY. Yes, sir; I think so.

The CHAIRMAN. Now, Mr. Secretary, we might as well pass along, perhaps, to those things which you have to say especially.

Secretary WILSON. Yes, sir. The Bureau of Animal Industry is the next section.

The CHAIRMAN. No; on page 8 of the section dealing with the Weather Bureau, line 7, you propose a change from " seacoast telegraph " to " Weather Bureau telegraph."

Secretary WILSON. Yes; they prefer the general term.

Doctor GALLOWAY. It used to be that the Weather Bureau had control of all the seacoast telegraph, but it does not now under the present system, so that Professor Moore wants to put that limiting phrase in there: " Weather Bureau telegraph, telephone, and cable lines."

Senator HANSBROUGH. That makes it uniform, Mr. Chairman. I think it had better be changed.

The CHAIRMAN. Yes; I do not see any objection to the change. As I understand it, you think it would not be available for repairs of a seacoast line. What does a seacoast line mean?

Secretary WILSON. The lines along the seacoast nowadays belong to several Departments of the Government, and I suppose they want to distinguish as between ours and others by calling ours the Weather Bureau telegraph.

The CHAIRMAN. You have telegraph lines of your own?

Secretary WILSON. Oh, yes, sir; a good many of them.

Senator WARREN. I should think that would be proper.

The CHAIRMAN. Yes. Now, in line 11.

Senator FRAZIER. What page are you on, Mr. Chairman?

Secretary WILSON. Page 8. In line 11 it is proposed to employ, for part of our work, officers in other Departments. For example, for doing some of our work along the seacoast we can employ for a small amount officers of the Navy Department, of the Marine Corps, etc., to take observations for us, and this gives us authority to do it for very small amounts.

Senator PERKINS. Men employed at life-saving stations, and so on?

Secretary WILSON. Yes, sir; all these things. Where some other Department of the Government happens to have a man already, he can take observations for us for a very small increase in his salary.

Senator PERKINS. We have established this year on the coast of Oregon and Washington some three or four different life-saving stations. You can obtain their services for a mere nominal sum, and you certainly should have the authority to do so.

Secretary WILSON. That is what that means.

The CHAIRMAN. The general law forbids the payment of two salaries, you know, to any Government officer.

Senator MONEY. What you want is to permit the officers to receive these sums, and you to pay them? You want both?

Doctor GALLOWAY. Yes, sir; we have not that clause.

Senator MONEY. You must have both. They will have to have permission to receive it, too, Mr. Secretary, I think. I agree with you. I think you ought to have it, but I think you ought to have something permitting them to receive it, should you not?

Doctor GALLOWAY. That is true, Senator. This clause has not been fully worked out. It might read " who may be employees of other Departments of the Government, and who may receive additional compensation."

Senator MONEY. Have you got that in there?

Doctor GALLOWAY. No, sir.

Senator MONEY. I think you had better put that in, because otherwise we would be limiting the authority to paying it.

Doctor GALLOWAY. When Doctor Moore discussed the matter with me he was more anxious for authority to employ them than anything else, and I do not think the question of pay was troubling him at all. He recognized, however, the necessity for authority to give additional compensation.

Senator MONEY. That is not the point. The point is that you propose to pay these people some sum, some little trifling sum. Now, they can not receive it under the law, and if you just insert there a provision that they can receive it you will have what you want.

Doctor GALLOWAY. Professor Moore says, for example, that he could get a man connected with one of the other Departments to do for $10 a month what would otherwise require an expert sent out especially to do that work at $75 a month.

Senator MONEY. That is all right. I am simply trying to carry out the Secretary's idea by authorizing that man to receive pay.

Secretary WILSON. I think it would be well to put that in.

Senator WARREN. We can add that provision, that they can re·ceive compensation in addition to their regular salaries.

Senator PERKINS. I think, Mr. Secretary, that if you will prepare an amendment that may be inserted there.

Secretary WILSON. Very well; we will do that.

Senator MONEY. Just allowing him to receive it; that is all.

Senator FRAZIER. Otherwise he can not do it.

Senator MONEY. No; it would be forbidden by law.

Secretary WILSON. I think what is in Professor Moore's mind is that in a great many cases they can get these men without additional compensation. They can get their services for nothing. That was his original idea, I think, but this suggestion of yours is a good one, and that should go in there.

The CHAIRMAN. On page 9, line 16, you ask for an auditor for the Bureau of Animal Industry.

Secretary WILSON. In every one of our bureaus we have a bureau auditor, who takes up the accounts of the bureau as they come in and ascertains whether the money has been expended according to the authorization and the law and all that. The Bureau of Animal Industry have never had one. They have had their work done with clerks; and I would like them to have an auditor, because while the accounts of all the bureaus and officers and divisions go to the disbursing officer with his auditors before they finally go to the Treasury Department, yet, at the same time, the auditors in the disbursing officer's office do not know all the details of the work in the several bureaus as well as an auditor within the bureau.

Senator MONEY. Mr. Secretary, I wish you would illustrate that. Name some item for which the auditor would have to account and have his account audited.

Secretary WILSON. We may send one of our people, perhaps, to travel over the packing houses, or to go out West and arrange for the inspection of animals in the fall time, when they are being shipped to the great centers, and we pay him a salary. He probably has an annual salary, and we pay his expenses to the extent of so much a day. If we send that man away up in the Northwest, he can probably live on $1.50 a day or $2 a day. If we send him down to New York, he goes to the limit of $5 a day, because it costs him more. Now, the men in that Bureau know more about the details of what it should cost and all those things than the man in the disbursing office does. We have that everywhere except in the Bureau of Animal Industry, and I think we ought to have it there.

Doctor GALLOWAY. It is not an increase in the grand total. We are simply taking it out of the lump sum—paying the man out of a lump sum.

Secretary WILSON. Yes; we want to pay him out of a lump sum. I want to have the accounts first audited in the Bureau, and then after that they go to the Auditor of the Department.

Senator MONEY. Do you have any returns from the experimental farm—butter or milk or cheese, or anything of that sort?

Secretary WILSON. We send out inspectors all the time under the law to ascertain whether the United States experiment stations have expended the $15,000 they get from Congress for research work. Their books are all looked over to see whether they have expended that money in that way, or whether they are using it for something outside of research. We look into that every year. The law requires it. They have to file their reports with us with regard to the use of that money before we can authorize the Treasury to pay them.

Senator MONEY. Now, Mr. Secretary, what I want to get at is this: Is there anything produced by the Department that is sold and the proceeds turned in?

Secretary WILSON. Along this line, we got authority a few years ago, in shipping meats, dairy products, and fruits to foreign countries to open up markets for our own people, to take the proceeds and use them over again. We have been doing that, and those moneys have been lying with the disbursing officer of the Department; and lately I have arranged to have all such moneys put into the United States Treasury.

Senator MONEY. Who handles that money? To whom does it come first?

Secretary WILSON. It is handled first by the disbursing officer of the Department.

Senator MONEY. Does he receive all the money?

Secretary WILSON. Yes; he receives it all.

Senator MONEY. Then who pays it to him?

Secretary WILSON. It is paid to him in this way: For instance, a commission man in London sells butter for us after it has been inspected—after we have gotten the lesson out of it that we want.

Senator MONEY. Your agent in London, then, sends that money directly to the disbursing officer?

Secretary WILSON. He sends it directly to the disbursing officer.

Senator MONEY. It comes directly to him, does it?

Secretary WILSON. Oh, surely.

Senator MONEY. And the account is audited by him?

Secretary WILSON. Oh, surely.

Doctor GALLOWAY. He is a bonded officer.

Secretary WILSON. We do not ourselves handle a dollar of it. It all comes through the hands of bonded officers. But heretofore it has been lying with our own disbursing officer; and I found after the legislation of last winter that moneys coming from the sale of timber were going to reach high amounts, and so arranged to have them all put into the Treasury just as fast as they came in instead of putting them in private banks here.

Senator MONEY. That is the point. There is a man who sells timber, for example. He pays the money in to your disbursing officer, and his account is audited there, is it?

Secretary WILSON. Yes.

Senator MONEY. By your disbursing officer?

Secretary WILSON. Surely; and it goes from there into the Treasury. It is not what you lawyers understand as "covered" into the Treasury. It is not in that shape at all. It is there subject to our drawing out. That is how it is there.

Senator LONG. It does not require an appropriation to get it out?

Secretary WILSON. No; it does not require an appropriation to get it out.

Senator MONEY. It is part of the current fund that you can use?

Secretary WILSON. Yes; that we can use.

Senator MONEY. All you want, then, is an auditor for this particular Bureau of Animal Industry?

Secretary WILSON. I want the first auditing done in the Bureau where the auditor has a knowledge of the field work.

Senator FRAZIER. In order to accomplish that, do you ask for an additional auditor, or will the force that you have answer?

Secretary WILSON. We will probably appoint an auditor there who has been doing that work.

Senator FRAZIER. But you do not ask for an additional sum of money?

Secretary WILSON. An additional sum of money—no.

Senator MONEY. It is an additional office.

Doctor GALLOWAY. The money is already there, and the Secretary only wants authority to employ the man. One other point in that connection, emphasizing what Senator Money has brought out, is this: The Bureau of Animal Industry, or any other bureau, sometimes finds it necessary to buy large quantities of technical apparatus, which has to be purchased in the open market; and the accountant should be familiar with that sort of work, which the accountants in the disbursing office are not always familiar with. He may get $10,000 worth of laboratory apparatus; and the auditing officer in the Bureau should be familiar with the cost and prices, contract prices, or competitive prices, so that he can use his intelligence in handling the accounts when they come in.

Senator MONEY. Let me ask you this question, as long as you have gone into that subject: Here is a man that sells timber, or butter, or whatever it is. What sort of an account does he render—how does he keep his books, for instance? What bookkeeping does he do?

Doctor GALLOWAY. Take the concrete case in which the Bureau of Plant Industry is handling fruit; we are opening the fruit markets to foreign countries. We purchase in the open market a certain amount of fruit, and it is sold in London. The check is made payable to the Pomologist in charge of the fruit work, and it comes to him. At the same time there is a detailed statement rendered to the disbursing office of the sales, expressage, freightage, icing, charges, and everything. That all comes in.

Senator MONEY. That is made by the agent?

Doctor GALLOWAY. That is made by the agent.

Senator MONEY. Now, that is the point that I want to know about—what kind of books those gentlemen keep who receive the money and transfer it to your disbursing officer, where their accounts, I presume, are all audited; what kind of books do those gentlemen keep who receive the actual cash from the sale of anything?

Doctor GALLOWAY. Speaking for the fruit work alone, those agents are in nearly all cases commercial agents, so that they have only the ordinary form of commercial bookkeeping to follow; but they must submit their accounts on specified forms provided by the Department, and their books must agree with those forms.

Senator MONEY. But they do keep the commercial bookkeeping accounts?

Doctor GALLOWAY. Yes, sir.

Senator MONEY. That is what I wanted to get at. I did not know how they kept their accounts, and I can see very well that there would be great trouble in auditing accounts that were not kept by regular bookkeeping methods—for instance, a lot of memoranda and one thing and another, loose papers, etc., and evidences of transactions.

The CHAIRMAN. On page 11, lines 23 and 24, there is a pretty large increase asked for in the general appropriation.

Secretary WILSON. This is a matter, gentlemen, about which I have been laboring with the House committee all winter. I have not sufficient money to inspect the animals on the ranges and at the packing houses. The whole world just now has its attention drawn to the quality of American meats. Magazine articles are written, books are written, etc., lying volubly about our inspection, but there are some facts to which your attention ought to be called.

I had not money' enough last fall to employ inspectors to inspect the cattle on the ranges before they were put in the trains, in the countries where the sheep have scab and the cattle have mange. I had not the money to do it. I had not, for six months last fall and winter, money enough to inspect meats at the packing houses. There is a great demand in foreign countries, especially in Germany, for our meats, and 18 houses wanted inspection that I could not give—18 houses. It is well known that by an understanding we had with Germany some years ago, when she had shut out our meats, we agreed to microscopically examine our pork. The Germans do not cook their meats as we do. Consequently the one and a fraction per cent of hogs that are found to have trichinæ might do mischief when they got to Germany, and we have been inspecting microscopically, and there are these 18 houses to which I could not give inspection. I wanted $135,000 more and the House gave me $20,000 more. The Senate put it up to what I wanted, and then, in order to get anything, the Committee on Appropriations of the Senate had to agree to split the sum in two, or something like that, with the Committee on Appropriations of the House.

Now, then, we have estimated what will be required for the work in the coming year. We are pretty well through with cleaning up the ranges with mange and scab. Moreover, as the country develops and grows, we are needing more packing houses to take care of the great farm and ranch and plantation products of meats. Consequently, we are needing more and more men to do that work; and we have made a careful estimate of so much money to do this work for us. Conditions change. The Pacific coast is filling up very rapidly. They do not grow corn there, consequently they can not grow their own hogs on the Pacific coast. They are putting up packing houses, and they take their hogs from the Mississippi Valley by the train load; but they insist that those hogs shall be inspected. We have not money to inspect them. Their laws will not let them in without inspection, and there you are. Now, we have not inspectors enough. If you want to have the very best work done in the packing houses that ought to be done for the health of the American people, we have not inspectors enough to do that work.

Senator MONEY. How much do you ask for?

Secretary WILSON. I am asking for our estimate, $104,000 more, or so much of it as I may need to get those inspectors.

Senator WARREN. You will remember, Mr. Perkins, that we had to provide in a deficiency bill for a large amount there; and then they got into conference and cut it down. They do not seem to be willing so far, in the House, to accept the situation. I do not think it is a matter that we can temporize with at all. I think we shall have to give the Secretary his estimate.

A A B—06——2

Senator Money. I think so, too.   I think he ought to have it.

Senator Perkins. I have not your estimate before me; but you are not asking for any more than your estimate?

Secretary Wilson. No; not a dollar more.

Here is a little proviso that I would like to have you put in at the end of the section dealing with the Bureau of Animal Industry, on page 14:

Provided, That the Secretary of Agriculture is authorized to purchase in open market samples of all tubercular serums, antitoxins, or analogous products, of domestic or foreign manufacture, which are sold in the .United States for the detection, prevention, treatment, or cure of diseases of domestic animals, to test the same, and to publish the results of such tests in such manner as he may deem best.

I will give you an illustration that will call your attention to what is going on.

Senator Perkins. Where do you wish that proviso to come in?

Doctor Galloway. At the end of the section dealing with the Bureau of Animal Industry, on page 14.

Secretary Wilson. One of the finest herds of Jersey cows that I ever saw in my life is found at Biltmore, down in North Carolina. They are always very anxious to have them very healthy, and so annually they have them tested with tuberculin to ascertain whether or not they have tuberculosis.   They got the tuberculin from commercial houses, and every year they found that the operations gave no results.   The indications were that the animals were entirely healthy.

When animals that have tuberculosis have tuberculin applied to them their temperature rises.   In this case there was no rise of temperature.   But they became suspicious, and sent up to us for some of our tuberculin; and they found that two-thirds of the largest herd reacted, fevered up, and showed that they had tuberculosis.

We have taken the matter up at our experiment station here on the edge of the District of Columbia and Maryland.   We have cows there that we know to be tuberculous.   We have tried that same tuberculin, and so forth, and it acts as it did at Biltmore.

Now, we would like to have authority here to do that kind of work and inquire into and test these things and find out to what extent the people of the United States are being deceived.   It is a very serious thing for a man who buys milk from his neighbor to get milk from a tuberculous cow.   If he is a great, strong man with a good, vigorous stomach, I am satisfied that he can probably digest all these things; but invalids and children, and so forth, do not.

Senator Money. You can not digest a germ.

Secretary Wilson. Exactly.   The scientists in my Department are satisfied that the animal tuberculosis affects the human family; and we think we would like to have that authority.

The next section is the Bureau of Plant Industry; and we happen to have Doctor Galloway here, and he will explain what little changes are made.

The Chairman. We will go now to page 15, the Bureau of Plant Industry.   Doctor Galloway, what do you ask for?

Doctor Galloway. We ask for an increase of two clerks there to take care of our normal growth.   We have about 150 or 200 clerks, and the Secretary this year in his estimate asked for an increase for clerk hire amounting to three or four thousand dollars, and they gave us about half of it in the House. We simply want to bring it up to the Secretary's estimate. That provides, in line 6, instead of 12 clerks, for making it 13 clerks of class 2.

The CHAIRMAN. Is it within the estimates?

Doctor GALLOWAY. It is all within the estimates; yes, sir. The total increase there aggregates less than $2,000.

Senator PERKINS. Did not the House give all you wanted, Doctor?

Doctor GALLOWAY. No, sir; we asked for an increase for clerk hire of about $4,800, and they gave us about $2,000.

Senator PERKINS. I am in favor of giving you all you want.

Doctor GALLOWAY. We have no authority anywhere else to engage clerks in the lump funds. We must get them in the statutory place. That simply represents our normal growth. That is, they gave increases in our lump funds, but not clerks to carry out the work under the lump funds.

The CHAIRMAN. You have increased the pay of the carpenter, I see.

Doctor GALLOWAY. We ask for $1,000 for this man. He has been there eight or nine years. We asked for $1,000 and the House gave us $900. He now gets $840. The House made it $900 and the Secretary estimated $1,000. We simply want to bring it up to the estimates. The House gave us about half what we asked for.

The CHAIRMAN. On the next page you have two " gardeners or assistants." Why do you put the words " or assistants " in there?

Doctor GALLOWAY. They come to us classified as " gardeners or assistants," and we can take them from the Civil Service either way then. We simply want authority to do that.

The CHAIRMAN. And you have increased the pay of the plumbers?

Doctor GALLOWAY. That was the same case as in the House.

The CHAIRMAN. Because they command more pay, I suppose?

Doctor GALLOWAY. They command more pay. We have only brought their wages up to about the ordinary pay of plumbers.

The CHAIRMAN. On page 17 you ask for more skilled laborers—an increase of three. That is doubling your present number.

Doctor GALLOWAY. We have those skilled laborers already. We have simply taken them out of the lump fund. We had them in the lump fund, and we have simply transferred them over there, and want the authority in the statutory place to carry them.

Senator WARREN. You do not reduce the lump fund that much, do you?

Doctor GALLOWAY. The lump fund was reduced originally, but it does not show in the bill, because there were some increase made in the House.

Senator WARREN. Yes; but if we make this increase here it increases the regular roll and leaves the amount the same in the lump sum; or do you want to deduct it from the lump sum?

Doctor GALLOWAY. We can deduct it from the lump sum.

The CHAIRMAN. On page 18 an amendment is pasted in here.

Doctor GALLOWAY. We have had that authority for a good many years, and that is the authority under which we do all of our important fruit work—that is, the shipping of fruit and the opening of new markets. That went out on a point of order in the House, but they did not object to this portion of it. They objected to the use of the money in rebuying the fruit, so they eliminated that part of it. We simply want authority to purchase the fruits and to turn the money back into the Treasury after the market has been established in accordance with the usual practice.

Senator WARREN. All the money that you will turn back from all these sales goes into the Treasury, but does not become an available fund for you?

Doctor GALLOWAY. No, sir; we formerly had that authority, and that went out on a point of order on the ground that it was commerce——

Senator WARREN. Do I understand you rightly that this makes no difference with your appropriation at all?

Doctor GALLOWAY. No, sir.

Senator WARREN. Whatever you buy you consume that much of your appropriation, for which you get no reimbursement?

Doctor GALLOWAY. No reimbursement.

Senator WARREN. Everything you sell goes into the Treasury straight?

Doctor GALLOWAY. It goes into the Treasury; yes.

The CHAIRMAN. That conforms to the general principle that has been the general principle for a good while, but with a good many exceptions. The exceptions are being eliminated now. The rule is that everything received from any source shall go into the Treasury, and shall not be taken out except on regular appropriations.

Doctor GALLOWAY. The whole thing does not amount to but about $3,000 a year so far as we are concerned. In fact, we handle a very small part of it.

Senator PERKINS. As you are aware, Mr. Chairman, there has been a good deal of criticism in the Senate, and certainly in our Committee on Appropriations, as to the business policy of permitting any Department of the Government to have a fund of its own and to cover it in the Treasury and withdraw it without its being audited by the general Auditor of the Treasury Department. You will remember that a resolution was offered some few days since, I think by Senator Heyburn, of Idaho, in which the action of the Bureau of Forestry in selling timber for which we received large sums of money was criticised.

Senator WARREN. For grazing.

Senator PERKINS. For grazing; and it was paid out without being audited, so it was charged. I do not think that such a course meets your approval generally, nor do I·think it is the proper principle to give the different Departments of the Government power to do that.

Senator HANSBROUGH. We have a bill now, Senator Perkins, coming from the Committee on Public Lands, dealing with that subject.

Senator PERKINS. As you know, in all the corporations of the country—certainly in the railroad and banking and other corporations with which I have been connected—such money must go through the regular business course prescribed by the rules of the company, and I think that as a general proposition it is the safe course to pursue. I am only speaking in a suggestive way, because I certainly have no adverse criticism to pass upon your Department, and certainly not on Doctor Galloway, for he is one of the most efficient and capable men, I think, in the Government employ.

In other words, Doctor, I think you should have such a financial system devised that there can be no adverse criticism made upon it.

Doctor GALLOWAY. That is exactly what we have here. We buy this fruit in the market, just as if we were going out to buy any other thing in the market, and the accounts are rendered in the ordinary way, as Government accounts; and when the fruit is sold the money is turned into the Treasury, and must be reappropriated by the Government for further use.

(The committee thereupon adjourned until to-morrow, Tuesday, May 8, 1906, at 10 o'clock a. m.)

COMMITTEE ON AGRICULTURE AND FORESTRY,
UNITED STATES SENATE,
Washington, D. C., Tuesday, May 8, 1906.

The committee met at 10 a. m.

Present: Senators Proctor (chairman), Hansbrough, Warren, Dolliver, Perkins, Money, Simmons, Frazier, and Latimer.

Present, also, Hon. James Wilson, Secretary of Agriculture; Dr. B. T. Galloway, Chief of the Bureau of Plant Industry, Agricultural Department, and Gifford Pinchot, esq., Forester and Chief of the Bureau of Forestry, Agricultural Department.

STATEMENT OF HON. JAMES WILSON—Continued.

(The chairman stated that before taking up the bill where the committee left off yesterday, the committee would go over the items struck out of the bill in the House of Representatives on points of order.)

The CHAIRMAN. Please refer to page 19 of the original bill.

Secretary WILSON [reading]:

And such fruits, vegetables, packages, and packing materials as are needed for these investigations and experimental shipments may be bought in open market and dispensed of at the discretion of the Secretary of Agriculture, and the money received from the sale of such fruits, vegetables, packages, and packing materials shall be deposited in the Treasury of the United States.

The CHAIRMAN. You do not consider that important?

Doctor GALLOWAY. We do not consider it important, Senator; but we would like to have some authority to put the money back into the Treasury, but not use it over again.

Secretary WILSON. We would like to do that work. It is of exceedingly great importance.

Doctor GALLOWAY. That, of course, would mean that we would handle all those accounts in the usual governmental way, and the money would be turned into the Treasury, in accordance with the usual custom, and not used over again.

Secretary WILSON. There is an amendment here; you will find an amendment on page 18.

The CHAIRMAN. But how important do you consider it that you should be allowed to do the work?

Doctor GALLOWAY. It is only of minor importance. We would like to do it; but if you think it is best, just eliminate it; take it out.

The CHAIRMAN. I am ascertaining whether it would be held subject to a point of order in the Senate, but I thought I would like also to know how important it is to you.

Secretary WILSON. I think there has been a great deal of help given to fruit people throughout the United States by sending our fruit over there and showing them how to pack it, and all that; but it is not of enough importance to make any great ado about. We can help those people anyway about the shipments.

The CHAIRMAN. On page 28 of the original bill, Bureau of Chemistry, line 11, they strike out the language beginning with "to investigate the adulteration, false labeling," etc., clear down to the word " use " in the second line on the twenty-ninth page.

Secretary WILSON. A few years ago there were a couple of lines put in the appropriation bill authorizing us to inquire into the adulteration and misbranding of foods and drinks coming from foreign countries, and with that authority we have substantially stopped the whole business. As soon as the American merchant found that he was handling adulterated or misbranded goods he notified his correspondents on the other side of the Atlantic that he did not want that kind of goods any more. We have stopped that whole business, gentlemen, without a suit in court. They have never gone to court to contest our findings. There is a pretty extensive line of work there. I can give you an illustration, the very last one we were troubled with.

They have ducks in China by the million on the great rivers, and every now and then there will be an egg broken, and they throw that into a receptacle by itself. It would not keep, of course, so they put borax in there to prevent the bacteria from multiplying and spoiling the eggs. Then they bring them over here and sell them to our bakers, and we eat the cake made from that borated egg product from China.

Now, we have insisted that if they put something in those eggs which was regarded as absolutely deleterious to health they must stop it, and if the product was misbranded they must brand it correctly, so that the people would know what they were buying. That was the last case we had. There was a good deal of kicking on the part of the man that had those eggs; but we stopped that, and the whole thing has stopped.

Senator PERKINS. Will borax stop fermentation?

Secretary WILSON. Oh, yes; that is what a preservative means. It means to stop the growth of bacteria; that is what it means. That is what salt is for.

Senator MONEY. Boracic acid is used in sausages and such things as that, too, is it not?

Secretary WILSON. Oh, surely; sausages and everything of that kind. They use salicylic acid also.

The fact of the matter is that you can keep things indefinitely if you have the temperature low enough. There are several ways of keeping things. You can dry them so that they will keep.

Senator PERKINS. Bacteria are not affected by cold, are they?

Secretary WILSON. Oh, yes. When you bring the drying of an article down to a certain point the bacteria can not multiply. They must have moisture and they must have heat and they must have oxygen generally.

Senator PERKINS. I saw some investigations recently where meat had been in cold storage, and while the fermentation and decay had been arrested, yet when it was exposed again the bacteria were found alive.

Secretary WILSON. There is this to be said also by the bacteriologists: They tell us that a certain kind of bacteria will develop after a long time in cold conditions, but the generality of bacteria are those that develop in warm conditions.

Senator MONEY. They develop by heat, but they are not killed by cold. You can preserve a yellow-fever germ in a block of ice indefinitely.

Secretary WILSON. Yes; that is true as to some of them. Take the kind of bacteria that fall into the milk pails when you milk the cow; that kind is developed by heat and can not develop with cold at all.

The CHAIRMAN. Then, Mr. Secretary, what would be the effect of this clause being left out?

Secretary WILSON. If you leave this clause out, the effect will be that all this business will begin again.

Senator MONEY. I want to ask you a question there. We have passed a pure-food bill through the Senate, and it has gone to the House, and they have struck out everything after the enacting clause and put in another bill. Day before yesterday—or Saturday, I think—they set a date for the hearing of that bill. What is the use of carrying along legislation for the same purpose in two separate bills? Here is a pure-food bill that includes this very thing, and here is this agricultural appropriation bill which includes the same thing.

Senator LATIMER. Senator Money, just one statement that probably you have not thought about, or perhaps you have: That bill is not yet enacted into law. They are trying to accomplish what we are trying to accomplish through that bill. In case that bill fails to pass, they can go under this bill, and in case it does pass it is under the same bureau. The enforcement of the bill that we passed in the Senate is under Doctor Wiley, as I understand it.

Senator MONEY. Well, in legislation it is a good plan to have an alternative bill in case another one fails.

Secretary WILSON. That is a matter which I suppose you gentlemen will determine in executive session.

Senator SIMMONS. This bill is going to pass. We know that. The other bill may not pass.

The CHAIRMAN. Now, Mr. Secretary, on the following page the clause in regard to establishing standards of purity for food products is also stricken out.

Secretary WILSON. Yes.

The CHAIRMAN. Do you consider that an important provision?

Secretary WILSON. Yes; we were just considering that clause down here—" to establish standards of purity for food products and to determine what are regarded as adulterations therein." I can give you an illustration of one of the standardizing acts. They have standardized butter, and determined what it should be. Among other things, it must not have more than 16 per cent of moisture.

I think we have natural jurisdiction of agricultural food products, and I think we should say to the world what butter is, what it should be. I remember distinctly that we have determined, in standardizing butter, that it must not have more than 16 per cent of moisture; it must not have more than that. Good butter does not have that much. First-rate butter does not have that much, but when they go beyond that it is regarded as adulterated. People are being cheated with regard to that, and with regard to meats; and we want to determine what shall be considered good meats, what shall be considered good grains, and the composition, etc., of the several grains.

Senator FRAZIER. How do you determine that, Mr. Secretary, and get the benefit of it to the people? Do you take dairy and other products and investigate them?

Secretary WILSON. I was authorized to appoint a committee of gentlemen to determine these standards, and did so. I appointed a committee of experts, and they sit down carefully and correspond with other experts all over the United States; and after they have gotten all the light they can possibly get on a subject they make a standard.

Senator SIMMONS. Mr. Secretary, after you have made that standard, what is its effect? You publish it to the country and that is the end of it, is it not?

Secretary WILSON. It is published to the country and that is the end of it.

Senator FRAZIER. It is simply a matter of information to the people.

Secretary WILSON. I suppose in the courts it would be prima facie evidence of the right thing, perhaps; I suppose so.

Senator HANSBROUGH. Mr. Secretary, to what extent would these proposed amendments of yours on page 30 interfere with what is known as the pure-food bill in case it should become a law?

Secretary WILSON. In case it should become a law I suppose it would cover the same points; but I do not think your pure-food bill does cover the standardizing.

Senator HANSBROUGH. No; it was the purpose of those who were interested in securing its passage to avoid establishing standards.

Secretary WILSON. Yes.

The CHAIRMAN. And that you consider important, that a standard should be established?

Secretary WILSON. I think so. I think the man who goes to the market to buy a pound of butter ought to be protected against getting 25 per cent of water.

Senator MONEY. Before we pass on this I think we had better have before us the House bill, which is substituted for the Senate bill.

The CHAIRMAN. Mr. Secretary, on page 30 of the old bill, lines 15 to 17, the words " or which are kinds of products excluded from any foreign country for any cause whatever " were stricken out.

It reads: " Or which are kinds of products excluded from any foreign country for any cause whatever when coming from this country." The point of that is that we will exclude from coming to this country from any foreign country whatever they would exclude if going from here to them.

Secretary WILSON. Yes.

The CHAIRMAN. It is a measure of retaliation. It does not strike me that it is important, for the reason that it is not because they exclude it that we want to, but we want to exclude what is not fit to come anyway, whether they do or not.

Secretary WILSON. We have that authority in this other place.

Doctor GALLOWAY. It is not important, Mr. Chairman. When this matter was submitted to Doctor Wiley he made the point that that could be just as well omitted and it would not make any difference.

The CHAIRMAN. The point they made in the House, which was sustained by the Chair (Mr. Wadsworth not contending for it in most cases)—the point they made in regard to a good many of these things was this: That although the provisions had been in the bills for years (some of them, I think, as long as ten years), yet, as they were only annual in their application, they were not law, and therefore putting them in again was new legislation. And under that ruling they shut out a good many provisions that had been right along in the bill year after year.

Secretary WILSON. I think those rulings, in view of the broad jurisdiction that the Department of Agriculture has under the organic act, were all wrong.

Senator WARREN. According to the way we have construed heretofore, new legislation has been that which we did not have before; and if we legislate in just what we had before they will surely not rule it out here. Some of them, though, are not in that class, I suppose.

The CHAIRMAN. They are almost all old matters that have been in the bill right along, without objection.

On page 31 of the old bill, if you will look at it, the whole proviso is stricken out that no payment for storage, cartage, etc., shall be made. The proviso begins in line 15. Is that an important matter, Mr. Secretary? It struck me that that would not be very important. You would reach the same result without it, would you not?

I should think that was a provision for the benefit of the owner of the goods.

Secretary WILSON. That is what it is for.

The CHAIRMAN. And I should not suppose it was important to the Department.

Secretary WILSON. I do not think it is important.

The CHAIRMAN. No. Now, I believe all that is left is on page 50— " Nutrition investigations."

Secretary WILSON. I think that is an incorrect ruling. We want to find out the digestibility of farm products, for example, and we take them up one after another; and there has been an immense amount of work done that is exceedingly valuable to the country. We have cooperated with experiment stations and colleges throughout the country to get that done; and if that can be stricken out on a point of order I think the most of the bill can go out on points of order at any time.

Senator MONEY. I have several letters, Mr. Secretary, from college presidents and university people about that. Since it was stricken out in the House these communications have come to me to see if it could not be restored.

Secretary WILSON. Oh, it ought to be restored, of course.

Senator MONEY. I received quite a number, three or four, this morning—one of them from Illinois.

Secretary WILSON. We have no right, without that, to conduct this work. They put a man into a calorimeter to ascertain how much he gets in the way of nutrition from what he eats. They ascertain how much food he gets, and that is reduced to the different elements. An ascertainment is made of how much that man eats of all the different elements of food.

Then a note is taken, by one of the finest machines in the world, of where it all goes, and then they ascertain the effect of food on the human being.

The CHAIRMAN. You consider that a very important provision?

Secretary WILSON. Oh, very—exceedingly important.

The CHAIRMAN. Now, we have had the view of the Secretary upon these points. We will go back now to where we left off yesterday morning.

Senator MONEY. Mr. Chairman, before we go back I want to invite your attention to page 29 of the old bill. If that part remains out which has been ruled out there, I believe from line 14 down to part of line 16, "adulterations therein," then the two lines and a half above that should go out, too, because they depend upon that, and are left standing in the air. As a matter of fact, that language was included in the motion to strike out, but by inadvertence it was left in. I ascertained that by inquiry. I saw it standing in the air there with no relation to anything else if this was stricken out below, and the gentleman who made the motion told me that he moved to strike out all of that, but through some inadvertence it was left in.

Senator FRAZIER. That begins, then, at line 11, does it?

Senator MONEY. Yes, sir; at line 11, the latter part—"to enable," etc.

The CHAIRMAN. After the word "countries?"

Senator MONEY. Yes, sir. If the latter part goes out, that should go out, too, for it has no relation to anything otherwise.

The CHAIRMAN. You are right about that. That was left in the bill by mistake. The point of order included that, but it was put in, I suppose, by inadvertence.

Senator MONEY. That is the case; that is so.

The CHAIRMAN. But I do not know that we need to go into that matter. It is all right to leave it in.

Senator HANSBROUGH. Mr. Secretary, in view of the probable enactment into law of the pending pure-food bill, do you not think it would be a good idea to avoid the establishment of standards at the present time until that law comes before you, as it probably will?

Secretary WILSON. The new food bill does not cover the question of standards.

Senator HANSBROUGH. Well, that is it. The question arises whether, if the bill becomes a law, it would be desirable for this Department to establish standards?

Secretary WILSON. Oh, I think so. They have never been established. I think so. It is my judgment that standards ought to be established.

Senator HANSBROUGH. I am very much afraid you will have a great deal of difficulty in persuading the Senate that the establishment of standards in an appropriation bill would not be new legislation.

Secretary WILSON. Well, that is your work. It is probably more difficult to justify that one thing than anything else, and yet they are standards with regard to agricultural products.

Senator HANSBROUGH. And if you got started on a system of establishing standards through provisions in an appropriation bill, and then a pure-food bill should come to you which avoided the establishment of standards, you would have some difficulty in readjusting yourself to the new law.

Secretary WILSON. I suppose if there are no standards mentioned in the food bill and the thing is stricken out here it would stop standardizing altogether. That is what it would do. The question is whether it is desirable to stop it.

Senator HANSBROUGH. Meantime you would set up your machinery to establish standards?

Secretary WILSON. Oh, yes; the machinery has been going for years. There is no doubt about that. We have standardized a good deal.

Senator HANSBROUGH. But all that would have to be stopped? You would have to drop it?

Secretary WILSON. If this is left out, we would simply have to stop standardizing after the 1st of July.

Senator LATIMER. Mr. Secretary, what effect has the decision of the Department over here as to adulteration had on the market of any product that has been shipped to the United States?

Secretary WILSON. It has stopped the importation of all the adulterated and misbranded goods. That is what it has done.

Senator LATIMER. Have you had any complaints from parties who were shipping products that were misbranded, where they proved to be injurious to health and you have passed upon them? Has there been much complaint in that line?

Secretary WILSON. There have been a few people who have complained. In the case of the duck eggs that I was telling you about they have complained about our stopping that, but they did not feel like going into court about it.

Senator PERKINS. Mr. Secretary, do you not think that a very large percentage of imported olive oil is adulterated?

Secretary WILSON. We have found it so.

Senator PERKINS. Do you not think so at the present time?

Secretary WILSON. We have stopped all the importations of adulterated olive oil.

Senator MONEY. Mr. Secretary, I venture to say that there are not half a dozen bottles of olive oil in this town right now.

Senator PERKINS. I mean pure olive oil.

Senator MONEY. The Italian Government absolutely prohibited the importation of cotton seed or cotton-seed oil, upon the ground that it destroyed the olive industry.

Secretary WILSON. Yes.

Senator MONEY. But after a while they repealed that law and the cotton-seed oil has gone in there, and it is refined, and I will defy anybody on earth to tell the difference. You may have a chemical analysis that will detect the difference.

Secretary WILSON. I agree with you that cotton-seed oil, well refined, is just as nice as olive oil; but we want the people to get what they think they are getting.

Senator PERKINS. I venture to say that you can demonstrate what I have said by your chemists—that you can go into any grocery store in this city, or almost any other city, and unless it is California olive oil you will not get any pure olive oil that is imported.

Secretary WILSON. Very likely.

Senator PERKINS. Then how do you standardize it?

Secretary WILSON. It is not a question of standardizing as far as that is concerned. We have not undertaken to standardize that. We have undertaken to stop the importation of adulterated olive oil.

Senator PERKINS. But it is coming in in every shipment that comes here.

Secretary WILSON. Oh, we have substantially stopped the whole thing.

Senator SIMMONS. Mr. Secretary, do you mean to say, then, that this cotton-seed oil that we buy under the label of olive oil is not imported into this country, but is produced here in this country?

Secretary WILSON. What there is now is produced in this country, and my impression is that if you would sell it for just what it is, it would be found to be just as good oil as can be gotten anywhere.

Senator WARREN. Is not cotton-seed oil for table use manufactured largely in this country right now?

Secretary WILSON. Yes; but they take it over there into foreign countries, and they adulterate their olive oils with it and send them here as olive oil. Then they take the peanut oil that is grown in Egypt and adulterate the olive oils with it and send them over here: but our chemists can find them out. They can detect the whole thing, and they have stopped all that kind of business.

The CHAIRMAN. Senator Perkins, is it not possible that that adulteration is mainly done in this country?

Senator PERKINS. Oh, you will find that adulterated product coming from the custom-houses to-day in every invoice of oil that comes in. Of course it is branded olive oil; it is branded in the Italian language or French language with the name of the oil, the particular brand; but it is not pure olive oil.

Secretary WILSON. If they brand it for just what it is, it comes in; but they must brand it for just what it is.

Senator PERKINS. They all give it a particular name, a peculiar name. When I have been merchandizing I have imported myself thousands and thousands of cases of it, and some of it was branded olive oil, but since then they have changed the name. It is the same facsimile, however. Of course if it is branded pure oil, as you say——

Secretary WILSON. The American merchants have all stopped bringing in these adulterated and misbranded things. They have all stopped it. We have no trouble with them at all. If you stop looking into these importations, of course they will all begin over again. You will get the duck eggs in your cake, and so on.

The CHAIRMAN. There is almost no pure maple sirup for sale any more. I went, a couple of years ago, to every grocery house in town and did not find any. Since then one house has bought some genuine sirup. It is usually made with some maple sirup and cane sirup melted with it. If there is a short crop of maple sirup they put in more cane sirup.

Secretary WILSON. Up to date, Senator, we have had no jurisdiction of these things made within the United States—none whatever.

Senator WARREN. The State laws are after some of them.

Secretary WILSON. The State laws are after them to some extent.

Senator WARREN. My State is having a whole lot of fun along that line.

The CHAIRMAN. Now, Mr. Secretary, to get back to the regular order, on page 20 you ask for an increase of $25,000 for the investigation of harvesting, curing, transporting, storing, and marketing of fruits and vegetables.

Secretary WILSON. Yes, sir. We have a corps of people over there now, and the people on the Pacific coast tell us they are doing them untold good by helping them. They are studying fruit from the tree. Doctor Galloway probably can tell you more about that than I can.

Doctor GALLOWAY. Mr. Chairman, for two or three years we have been investigating the question of the loss of fruit in transit. We began our work in the South, on perishable fruits like peaches, determining the causes of the loss in transit in shipments to the north. Then we took up the citrus fruits of the Pacific coast, and we have for two years been working out there. Last year we spent only a small sum of money, two or three thousand dollars, but the growers of citrus fruits in southern California estimated that the saving that resulted during last year alone was $200,000.

We have asked this year for an increase in that work, so that we can not only take up the citrus fruit shipments but the deciduous fruits as well. The Secretary in his estimates asked for $25,000, which the House did not allow, and we are asking here that it be put back, so that we can enlarge the scope of the work and take up the deciduous fruits of the Pacific coast and the deciduous fruits of other sections of the country in addition to the citrus fruits. The question involves the interests of the producer of fruits and the interests of the packer of fruits and the interests of the consumer of fruits.

Senator PERKINS. I have quite a number of telegrams and I have here 50 letters. I do not want to weary you with them.

The CHAIRMAN. When we come to executive session perhaps it will be well to have some of those telegrams printed in the report.

Senator WARREN. How about that proviso on page 20? There is no occasion for inserting that, is there?

Doctor GALLOWAY. No; we do not need that in here.

It was put in by a member on the floor of the House to have some work done down in southern Missouri. We are doing that work anyway now.

Senator PERKINS. In connection with this section which we have been discussing the appropriation included an amount sufficient for you to investigate the pear blight, did it not? Mr. Wadsworth said he had increased that amount.

Doctor GALLOWAY. It was not increased, Senator, by the committee at all. They did not give us the estimates; but in the scramble which took place on the floor of the House for the seed business Mr. Wadsworth put back $76,000, which goes right into our general fund, and we can use part of that for that purpose.

Senator PERKINS. That is what Mr. Wadsworth said to me—that he was in favor of the proposition, and he would give you the money in a lump sum. In connection with that, Mr. Secretary, if you please, you have been giving the hop investigation—the disease of the hop vine—some consideration, and you can use that money for that purpose, can you not?

Secretary WILSON. I think we can.

Senator LATIMER. When the provision is made about seeds, that so much shall be spent in that way, I suppose it will have to be done.

Doctor GALLOWAY. Yes; but we have provided for that. There will be the same amount of seed as before; but in the House committee originally they cut out the seed proposition and put back $76,000 for forage crops and things of that kind; and while they put back the money for the forage crops and cotton, and put on another $76,000, it will enable us to do this pear-blight work and other work.

Senator FRAZIER. Doctor, before you leave this fruit section here, what is the purpose of those investigations, and how do they result in material benefit to the raisers, shippers, and consumers of fruit?

Doctor GALLOWAY. Take, for example, the concrete case of the peach growers in Georgia, the citrus growers in California.

Senator FRAZIER. Have you been investigating the peach crop in Georgia—the peach growers there?

Doctor GALLOWAY. Yes. We found, for example, that they lose anywhere from 15 to 25 per cent of their fruit in transit from Georgia to New York. Now, the points that we were investigating were as to how we could prevent those losses in transit. The questions there have to do largely with the determination of the prehandling of fruit—that is, the handling of the fruit before it goes into the car, the methods of handling in the orchard, the methods of handling in the packing house, and the methods of handling this fruit before they put it into the car. We found that when the fruit was put into the car and cooled after it was put in the car the loss would be from 60 to 75 per cent. If it was precooled—that is, cooled down to 40° and then put in the car—the loss was only 5 per cent. So that under those investigations arrangements were perfected for cooling the fruit before it was put into the car, and then, by actual determination, having a man at one end where it was shipped and a man at the other end where it was received, we could determine the loss under these different and varying conditions.

Now, we want to carry out that same kind of work with other fruits—apples and deciduous fruits. We have done so with some of the citrus fruits.

We found, for example, in California, that some citrus fruits going from Riverside to New York would lose 40 per cent by rotting. That had always been attributed to different kinds of diseases. But our Mr. Powell, who was working there, found that the main trouble came from very slight injuries in the gathering of the fruit, in the clipper cuts. The orange is cut off with a little pair of clippers. In the hurried work it is the practice to clip so fast that there are slight indentations or cuts made just at the stem of the orange. Actual tests showed that clipper-cut injured fruit lost about 30 to 40 per cent in transit; and then, when the fruit was carefully collected, and the nonclipper-injured fruit was sent, we only lost 2 per cent. The practical point was, then, just how to avoid the clipper cuts. The simple thing to do was to turn up the points of the clippers; and when that was done the representative of one of the large firms out there estimated that it saved him nearly a hundred thousand dollars on one season's crop. Just the simple thing of having his gatherers turn up the points of the clippers, so that in clipping the fruit they would not inflict these little, almost microscopical injuries, resulted in that great saving.

The CHAIRMAN. I brought up an amendment of Senator Talia-ferro's in regard to the white fly; but it is not likely that we will have any entomologists here. Would it not be advisable to adopt a provision of that kind?

Secretary WILSON. Doctor Howard and I carefully studied all his work when I was making my estimates. We estimated what we thought we would need for his work. I think the House did not give him a dollar more than he had last year; and if you can give him his estimates, or a considerable portion of them, the white fly will be taken care of.

The CHAIRMAN. I saw that in Florida this winter and paid a good deal of attention to it. I saw carloads of oranges at Orlando that were almost worthless. I went into several packing houses, but the disorder had not reached other sections of Florida. In that section it did exist.

Senator MONEY. Mr. Secretary, there is just one belt in Florida that has that, and no other.

Senator PERKINS. I have some correspondence, Mr. Chairman, be-tween the governor of California and Mr. True in relation to hops and in relation to pear blight. He states here in this letter that there are 235,000 bales of hops produced in California alone, which is nearly half the consumption of hops in the United States, and Oregon and Washington produce half as much more. They only ask $5,000 for this purpose, and I want you to be sure, Mr. Secretary, that there is sufficient money here for that purpose. Otherwise I would feel that I ought to ask or urge the committee to give you the increase.

Secretary WILSON. There are very interesting side lights connected with the growing of hop roots for the Pacific coast. They had, some years ago, just one kind. They wanted the earlier and later varieties.

Senator PERKINS. Have you sufficient funds now, do you think, for this purpose, to investigate the subject as you desire?

Secretary WILSON. I think if you could leave me the amount the House left, $76,000, the Doctor can take care of that.

Senator MONEY. I want to mention the fact that the pear blight has absolutely destroyed all the orchards in my country. They have not any pears there at all. They have simply died out, and they do not replant them.

Doctor GALLOWAY. We are making, out in California, one of the most extensive campaigns in the pear blight matter that has ever been undertaken, and I believe we can eradicate it from the State.

Senator MONEY. My State raises what I consider the most delicious fruits I ever ate in my life, but we can not raise the pear. We have tried it repeatedly, and they blight just about the time they get to maturity, and do so apparently without any reason. I have tried cutting them down to the green. You know there is a black strip that runs in the center of the branches; and I have tried cutting away down, and in fact I have cut them down to the grass and let them spring up again, and I found they did tolerably well. Still the orchards that were planted there very extensively a few years ago, when the pear fever went over that country—some people put in 500 acres—have simply perished; and now no one pays any attention to that industry.

Senator PERKINS. Can this pear-blight disease be eradicated?

Doctor GALLOWAY. I think that as conditions exist on the Pacific coast we can eliminate it.

Senator PERKINS. Are not the conditions the same in Mississippi?

Doctor GALLOWAY. I think it can be eliminated to a large extent there by proper handling. The trouble there is that there has never been any systematic effort. We can not get, in Mississippi, the united support of the fruit growers as we can in California. There you have an organization that is almost perfect in its systematic working.

Senator FRAZIER. Have you made any investigations in the South, in Mississippi or Tennessee, as to the pear blight?

Doctor GALLOWAY. Yes, sir.

Senator FRAZIER. We have it in Tennessee; our pears are practically destroyed by it.

Doctor GALLOWAY. We have made some studies in Tennessee.

Senator FRAZIER. What is the result of your investigations down there? Can you eradicate it?

Doctor GALLOWAY. Our investigations up to this time show us that any individual fruit grower can keep pear blight out of his orchard if he goes about it in the proper way. It is wholly a question of proper trimming.

Senator LATIMER. By spraying?

Doctor GALLOWAY. No, sir; by surgery. It is a surgical treatment trimming the trees.

The CHAIRMAN. Now, Mr. Secretary, you ask for $3,500 for the roads in the Department grounds.

Secretary WILSON. I would like to have some experimentation carried on on the grounds there with oils.

The CHAIRMAN. Let me ask whether that is for the purpose of experimentation in the line of good roads entirely or because the grounds need it?

Secretary WILSON. The grounds are in a bad state.

Doctor GALLOWAY. They are muddy and almost impassable at times.

The CHAIRMAN. Very well. Now let us go on to page 21. Five thousand dollars additional is desired for the purpose of encouraging the matting industry. Have you anything to say in regard to that—the matting industry?

Secretary WILSON. Yes; I have a great desire to say something about that. I think Doctor Galloway has that matter on his tongue's end.

Doctor GALLOWAY. Mr. Chairman, in two minutes I can explain what this thing is.

On page 21 there is an item of $5,000 to be added to our foreign fund for encouraging the matting industry. In Maine there is a firm that has developed machinery for the manufacture of Japanese and Chinese matting. We import 1,000,000 yards a week of that material—about $5,000,000 worth a year. The matting is made from a rush, a kind of sedge that grows in low, damp lands and swamps. We have found a place in South Carolina where we can grow the rush; but the rush roots have to come from Japan. We have to get the roots; it can not be grown from seed. We have the machinery and the factory end of it developed, and all that we need to do is to ᵃᵃᵃᵘre enough roots to get a few farmers to go into the industry of supplying the factories in Maine; and we think that if we have $5,000 we can do that this next year.

Senator WARREN. Economically speaking, can we, with our higher-priced labor and possibly more expensive ways of manufacture, compete with the matting made over there?

Doctor GALLOWAY. Yes, sir. These gentlemen in Maine are now manufacturing large quantities of matting, but they import the material from China and Japan. They import the raw grass from China, and they find that they can compete with the Chinese and Japanese labor. A Japanese workman makes only a few yards of matting in a day. In Maine they make many yards in an hour with their machine, and they make a class of matting that is superior to the Chinese and Japanese material. And they can make it so that they can sell it at the same prices as the Chinese and Japanese matting.

Senator WARREN. That is very interesting.

Senator LATIMER. Where is that grown—on moist lands?

Doctor GALLOWAY. On the rice lands, Senator. On the abandoned rice lands of South Carolina, where we are trying to establish the plants.

Secretary WILSON. We will apply machinery to the harvesting of it, too.

Doctor GALLOWAY. We have a small amount of it there, but we can not get the roots. The Japanese do not want to let them go out of the country. We can get the seed, but the material does not come true from seed. We find in California and some other sections of the country native species which we believe we can develop. We want to get about 100,000 roots, and we will have to send a man over there quietly to get them; and it will take about that amount of money to get them out and to establish them in three or four places in the South in the hands of farmers who are willing to grow 3 or 4 acres. This Maine concern agrees to pay a good price for all that can be grown. We can grow about 5 or 6 tons on an acre after we get the roots.

The CHAIRMAN. On page 22 there is a slight provision with regard to packages, which is not important.

Senator HANSBROUGH. That is especially beneficent to South Carolina, is it not?

Doctor GALLOWAY. I think it is.

Senator WARREN. On page 21, line 22, I observe that they have changed the proportion of seeds and made it five-sixths instead of two-thirds.

Secretary WILSON. That is all right. I divide them up among you people anyhow; you may as well take them.

Doctor GALLOWAY. Mr. Chairman and Senator Warren, may I make a statement just there?

Senator WARREN. Yes.

Doctor GALLOWAY. I simply wanted to have it on record that the members and Senators will not get any more seeds, for the reason that they have been getting five-sixths for the last five years. They have not been getting any less.

Senator FRAZIER. What was the change that was made?

Doctor GALLOWAY. They changed it from two-thirds to five-sixths, but the Secretary has been giving the five-sixths without that clause in there.

The CHAIRMAN. On page 23 there is a proviso that $5,000 of this sum may be used for the erection of a laboratory at Chico, Cal. That is a matter that you think is important?

Secretary WILSON. I think that is necessary. We do not ask for any more money, but simply for the authority to do it.

The CHAIRMAN. Now we come to the forest service.

Senator HANSBROUGH. Mr. Chairman, before you pass from the Bureau of Plant Industry, I would like to ask the Secretary of Agriculture what he thinks about incorporating an additional provision with respect to grains?

Secretary WILSON. Do you mean grading grains?

Senator HANSBROUGH. Yes.

Secretary WILSON. Would it not be necessary, if you wanted us to do that, to have an independent act passed, so that we would have an organic law instead of something on an appropriation bill? You see, they may raise the point in the House that that is commerce and not strictly agriculture.

Senator HANSBROUGH. I do not care much about what they say in the House about it. It is simply a question of what we can get through in the Senate.

Doctor GALLOWAY. May I add a word here?

Senator HANSBROUGH. Yes.

Doctor GALLOWAY. The point, as I understand it, about the grain inspection, is this: We may divide the inspection work into two parts—first, the inspection itself, and second, work having for its object the establishing of grades of grain. We can do this work in our laboratories and establish standards. We have no standards at all at the present time, but we can establish them.

Senator HANSBROUGH. Can you do that under the authority of the provisions of this appropriation bill?

Doctor GALLOWAY. We can not do it under the authority we have now.

Secretary WILSON. I do not think so.

Doctor GALLOWAY. There is nothing to prevent us from taking these samples of grain and making examinations of them.

Senator HANSBROUGH. You are aware that two bills are pending before this committee on grain inspection—one introduced by my colleague, Senator McCumber, and another by Senator Carter. The one introduced by my colleague is very lengthy, and I am afraid it would be pretty difficult to get any action on that at present. There are some things in the Carter bill, however, that impressed me. How would a provision of this kind do, Mr. Secretary, in this bill— authorizing the Secretary of Agriculture, under such rules and regulations as he may establish, to examine and report upon the nature. quality, and condition of any sample, parcel, or consignment of seed or grain which has been submitted for that purpose and furnish a copy of the report to the person who submitted the seed or grain, and providing that the Secretary of Agriculture may charge for said examination and report a price which shall cover the expense involved, the money to be deposited by the Secretary of Agriculture in the United States Treasury?

Secretary WILSON. We can do that. Probably it would be well to have that done.

Senator HANSBROUGH. I wanted to get your view about it before you got through.

Doctor GALLOWAY. I think it would necessitate a small appropriation to inaugurate the work, because the money is to be deposited in the Treasury, and we can not use it over again.

Senator HANSBROUGH. How much do you think it would take, Doctor?

Doctor GALLOWAY. We estimated about $25,000 for the inauguration of the work.

Senator HANSBROUGH. I may say that something of that kind will be offered in the Senate, if the committee does not put it into the bill.

Doctor GALLOWAY. After we get the work started, of course the $25,000 will go back into the Treasury; but we would have to pay that much out to get the wheels going.

Secretary WILSON. We can do that, and perhaps we should.

The CHAIRMAN. Is that all?

Senator HANSBROUGH. That is all. I simply wanted an expression on that point before we left the Plant Industry provision.

Secretary WILSON. Yes; we can do that.

The CHAIRMAN. Now the forest service: That was largely revised from last year, I believe.

Secretary WILSON. I would be glad if you could give Mr. Pinchot a brief hearing on this matter. It is in his hands, and is so very new, and so many new things are coming up all the time, that I would be glad to have him have a hearing.

STATEMENT OF GIFFORD PINCHOT, ESQ., FORESTER AND CHIEF OF THE FORESTRY SERVICE, AGRICULTURAL DEPARTMENT.

Mr. PINCHOT. Mr. Chairman, there are just two things I want to speak of in addition to the specific changes in the bill. You will recall that a little more than a year ago the forest reserves were transferred to the Department of Agriculture. I want to make a short report to the committee on the situation there.

We have now a little more than 104,000,000 acres of forest reserves, of which 100 reserves are in the United States, 2 in Alaska, and 1 in Porto Rico. When the Land Office had charge of the reserves, the last full year they drew a revenue of $59,000 from that area. This year the Secretary has estimated, officially, that the revenue will be $581,000, and privately we think that it will run over $600,000. In other words, we are trying to get the forest reserves as rapidly as possible on a paying basis, so that the charge will be taken off the Treasury.

Last year's appropriation was $875,000. This year the total expenses are about $1,400,000.

Senator LATIMER. Where does the increase of revenue come from?

Mr. PINCHOT. It comes from the sale of products on reserves, Senator, of which I will speak in just a moment. We have authority for that in the act which made the transfer.

Senator PERKINS. Grazing lands?

Mr. PINCHOT. Grazing and timber and special privileges. The total effect on the Treasury for this year will be a saving of perhaps $200,000 over the total expense of forestry last year, although we have a very much larger area of forest reserves and a very largely increased force; and I estimate that in five years from the transfer the reserves will be at least self-supporting. The total revenue for this year, as I said, will be probably not less than $600,000, or 10 times what it was in the Land Office.

Senator WARREN. Mr. Pinchot, you have not received very much from grazing yet, have you?

Mr. PINCHOT. Yes; the grazing fund is coming in very rapidly.

Senator WARREN. That is payable in advance, is it?

Mr. PINCHOT. In advance.

Senator WARREN. And in that way you have executed a good many leases for the coming season?

Mr. PINCHOT. We have received about $300,000 from grazing already, and other sums are coming in very rapidly.

Senator LATIMER. Your expense, then, was a million dollars, and you got about $600,000 out of the forest reserves. Will not that be self-sustaining pretty soon, at that rate?

Mr. PINCHOT. I think inside of five years it will be self-sustaining.

Senator DOLLIVER. Do you sell timber off of these reserves?

Mr. PINCHOT. Yes, sir.

Senator DOLLIVER. Lumber?

Senator WARREN. They sell full-grown and dead timber mainly, I suppose.

Senator PERKINS. And you are replenishing the forests, are you not?

Mr. PINCHOT. We are cutting in every case so as to preserve the forests.

Senator PERKINS. Are you setting out new trees?

Mr. PINCHOT. On a very large scale. There is a very considerable area of the reserves that has no timber now. It used to have timber, but it has been removed by fire and otherwise, and much of this land is on very important watersheds, important for irrigation and for other purposes. We are going to replace that timber through planting processes, which will be larger than have ever been undertaken anywhere before, but we hope to have it cost the Government nothing at all because of the proceeds.

Senator WARREN. Are you confining the reforestation entirely to the forest reserves?

Mr. PINCHOT. No; we are encouraging private individuals very largely to replant.

Senator PERKINS. I noticed that nearly everything now in Japan in the way of forestry is that which has been planted.

Mr. PINCHOT. Yes. We are doing our best to get private individuals to plant all over the United States, and with some success: but we are doing our planting only on the Government lands, of course.

The other side of our work is that of trying to get private individuals to see that forestry is a profitable thing. Very much the larger part of all the forests of the United States are now and probably always will be in private hands, and unless the country is to suffer most severely from timber shortage, and that within a comparatively short time, too, private individuals will have to take the matter up.

Now, however well we may manage the forest reserves, that will not touch the whole question. There will be three or four times as much timber land outside, and we must persuade the private owner what is the fact, that it pays to practice forestry. We are being fairly successful in that. The best illustration, I think, of the view taken by the lumbermen—through whose hands the timber must all pass, practically—is that they have, through their national association, voted to raise $150,000 for a chair of lumbering in one of the forest schools, on the ground that they will have to practice forestry, and when they begin they want men who know lumbering as well as forestry, which of course is exactly what we want in the forest reserves, too. But I think it is fair to report progress both in the management of the reserves and in persuading the private owners that it is worth while for them to take up forestry on their own side.

Senator WARREN. On page 25 I see that the estimate was $500; the law was $500, and they have changed it to $1,000. Is that something that you wish?

Mr. PINCHOT. Yes; we found that the nursery buildings that we had to put up——

Senator WARREN. You found that there is a possibility of some building reaching above $500?

Mr. PINCHOT. We found that we had places where we would have to put up two buildings for $500 apiece, instead of one for $750.

Senator WARREN. That is desired by the Department, is it?

Mr. PINCHOT. That is desired by the Department; yes, sir.

Senator LATIMER. These are buildings for the keepers of the forests?

Mr. PINCHOT. Buildings for them and for the men who have charge of our nurseries, where we are raising the plants, the young trees to plant, and so on. We have now in the field in the neighborhood of a thousand men, mainly on forest reserves, who are occupied in protecting them and caring for them; and we want very much to house those men comfortably in cabins through the reserves, the essential thing being to get the very best possible class of men. We can get better men for less money to work on forest reserves than can be had for any other purpose that I know of. The men like the work. It is a very attractive life, and we are constantly finding good men who are willing to give up better paying positions to come into the reserves.

Senator WARREN. I suppose, however, that most of those cabins and buildings cost much less than $500?

Mr. PINCHOT. Most of them cost much less than $500. We simply have to buy window sashes and a few nails and things like that. The rangers put them up themselves.

Senator WARREN. They use half dugouts and half cabins often?

Mr. PINCHOT. Yes; quite often; but we want to have respectable quarters, clean places for the men to live in.

The additions on page 26, Senator—were they what you had in mind?

The CHAIRMAN. What additions do you want here?

Mr. PINCHOT. Beyond the bill as it is now printed here, sir, there are only two.

On page 27 I would like to change, on line 24, " other " to " condemned." It is simply to make the appropriation follow the practice, because it is interpreted that way.

The CHAIRMAN. Yes.

Mr. PINCHOT. And leave out " the money received from such sales to be deposited in the Treasury." That is done under existing law already and with the emergency appropriations.

The CHAIRMAN. You ask, too, to strike out the last clause—" the money to be received from such sales to be deposited in the Treasury ? "

Mr. PINCHOT. That is already covered by existing law, sir. We do that anyhow, and would do it whether that were in or not.

Then, on page 55, at the bottom, in the emergency appropriations at the back, the " Bureau of Forestry " ought to be changed to " Forest Service," to make it correspond with the title before.

The CHAIRMAN. Yes. Is that everything?

Mr. PINCHOT. That is everything, sir.

Senator DOLLIVER. Are you going to extend the Black Hills Forest Reserve?

Mr. PINCHOT. There is not much chance of the Black Hills Reserve being extended; no, sir.

Senator DOLLIVER. There is a very fine forest being destroyed down about Whitewood, almost within sight of the limits of your reserves.

Mr. PINCHOT. The difficulty is that almost all the land on the outskirts of the Black Hills Reserve has already passed into private ownership.

Senator WARREN. It is mining land largely, too, is it not?

Mr. PINCHOT. It is mining land very largely.

Senator DOLLIVER. I know one tract there that is being ravaged of trees in the most reckless way; roots and everything else. It overlooks the Centennial Valley. There are probably four or five thousand acres there that, I should judge, would be a very important addition to that forest reserve.

Mr. PINCHOT. Yes; but we have looked it up, Senator, and that is practically all in private ownership.

Senator PERKINS. Mr. Chairman, when we reach the discussion of this forest reserve in the Senate some of our friends who are not as favorably disposed as I think all of the members of the committee are to forest reservations may criticise the manner in which the receipts from grazing lands, the sale of timber and other special privileges in the reservations, are received and disbursed. I think, therefore, that it might be well for you to ask Mr. Pinchot to briefly explain to the committee, in order that it may go in the record, the manner of disposition that is made, how the receipts are accounted for, and the disposition of the same.

The CHAIRMAN. Yes. Mr. Pinchot, will you tell us about that? The general policy is that everything should be deposited in the Treasury and subject to appropriation.

Mr. PINCHOT. Yes, sir; and I do not think that general policy can be attacked. May I say that the act of February 1, 1905, which transferred the forest reserves, contained this section:

That all money received from the sale of any products or for the use of any land or resources of said forest reserves shall be covered into the Treasury of the United States; and for a period of five years from the passage of this act shall constitute a special fund, available until expended, as the Secretary of Agriculture may direct, for the protection, administration, improvement, and extension of the Federal forest reserves.

The reason I want to ask as strongly as possible that that provision may be allowed to stand is this: New reserves are now being created quite rapidly—at the rate of many millions of acres a year. It is entirely impossible for us to tell at the beginning of any year what area of forest reserves we shall have to look after before the end of that year; and it would be hopeless, I think, to come to Congress asking for an appropriation to cover reserves not yet created. In other words, if this somewhat irregular arrangement can be allowed to continue until we can get straightened around, until the reserves are made and we can begin to estimate with a fair degree of accuracy as to what we shall need, it will be very greatly in the interest of the service.

The CHAIRMAN. Now, Mr. Pinchot, let us go to page 26. What is the need of that provision, beginning at line 22, covering into the Treasury " in the manner provided by section 5 of the act of Congress," etc., which is the general law now? Why should it be reenacted?

Mr. PINCHOT. As you will see on the next page, Senator—page 27—it says:

And the fund created by that act shall be available, as the Secretary of Agriculture may direct, to make refunds to depositors of money heretofore or hereafter deposited by them in excess of amounts actually due to the United States.

When a man buys timber, the first thing we make him do is to pay for that timber in advance; but we estimate how much timber there is. We may find that there is not quite as much as was covered by the estimate. Then he has a little coming back to him, or he makes application for timber, and he deposits his money as a guaranty of good faith and asks us to advertise. We say: " No; we will not sell you that timber for that price." That happens very often. We say: " You have got to pay more." He says: " I will not pay more." But the United States then has the money that he put up with his bid. The Treasury has asked us to put in a special provision of this kind in order to make the refund unquestioned. The reason is this: Moneys that are paid into the Government are under two classes— unofficial moneys, or unearned moneys, which the United States has not finally earned, and official moneys. Now, what we have to do in a case of this kind is to keep a certain amount of money unofficial in order to cover these refunds. We prefer to put the whole thing into the Treasury at once—it is the safest and best way—and then have authority to make the refunds from the regular amount.

Senator PERKINS. Who audits those refunds?

Mr. PINCHOT. There is quite an effective system of audit. In the first place, there is a special fiscal agent in the forest service whose accounts are audited there by another section in the forest service. Then the accounts of both are gone over very carefully by the Secretary's financial inspector, who is chief disbursing clerk of the Department; and, finally, the whole thing is gone over by the Treasury officers, so that the special fiscal agent has three separate audits.

Senator PERKINS. And you think it just as effective as it would be if the Comptroller or Auditor of the Treasury Department had charge of the work, as is done in auditing the funds of the Navy and War Departments and other Departments of the Government?

Mr. PINCHOT. I think the thing is absolutely effective.

Senator PERKINS. The reason I emphasize this fact is that it has been criticised by some of our friends who have not been as friendly to this work as others.

Secretary WILSON. We went over all this thing not very long ago, and where we found that moneys were coming into the hands of officers of the Department outside of their bonds, for example, we arranged, as Mr. Pinchot has indicated, to have them all go into the Treasury—that is, the Treasury is the custodian instead of a local bank; and we have most thorough methods of auditing in our Departments now. Each bureau audits, to begin with, because it knows the facts. Then we have an auditor in the disbursing office, and he audits again; and then the Treasury audits, etc.

Senator PERKINS. Personally, I have no question of it, Mr. Secretary; but I wanted to give you this opportunity of explaining, so that the chairman and other members of the committee would have an opportunity to explain the matter if the question should arise in the Senate that it was a departure from the general policy and plan of the Government as to receiving and disbursing moneys.

Senator WARREN. How many funds have you in the Treasury?

Mr. PINCHOT. One.

Senator WARREN. I notice here this cooperative fund. It says here that " all moneys received as contributions toward cooperative work in forest investigations shall be covered into the Treasury, and shall constitute a special fund."

Mr. PINCHOT. That is a new provision, Senator.

Senator WARREN. That would make a new fund, would it not?

Mr. PINCHOT. That would make two; but at the present time we simply have the one.

Senator WARREN. You deposit in the Treasury none of these funds as official funds, then? They are all special?

Mr. PINCHOT. Oh, no; everything goes in from the forest reserves as a regular fund.

Senator WARREN. You mean the regular official fund, to be drawn out by anybody?

Mr. PINCHOT. No, sir; to be drawn upon by us under this authority.

Senator WARREN. I say, then, that is a special fund in that respect; it is only drawn on for your particular purpose?

Mr. PINCHOT. Yes.

Senator WARREN. Now, then, this cooperative business is going to make another fund, is it?

Mr. PINCHOT. That we have now, but it is not deposited in the Treasury. You see, when a man wants a working plat for cutting his timber properly, we make him pay for it. He puts up the money in advance, and we use it to pay our men. Now, it happens a great many times that we have to make a refund to him, because we have estimated that it will cost a little more than it does. That money is now deposited under bond in a local bank. We would a great deal rather put it in the Treasury and have it treated like the other one; and that is the object of this provision.

Senator LATIMER. If a man goes to cut the timber and does not get as much as you have estimated, he is entitled to a refund?

Mr. PINCHOT. He is entitled to a refund.

Senator WARREN. But still you have this smaller fund?

Mr. PINCHOT. We have this smaller fund, which is entirely separate from the forest reserve fund.

The CHAIRMAN. Now, Mr. Pinchot, on page 27 of our bill, do you not think that under this act of February 1 you would be authorized to make refunds to depositors of money heretofore or hereafter deposited by them in excess of amounts actually due the United States? It would seem to me that all of this provision beginning with line 21 on page 26, at the end of that line, "and hereafter all moneys received," etc., down to "the United States," on line 8 of page 27, was unnecessary; that it was covered by the act of February 1.

Mr. PINCHOT. Mr. Senator, this suggestion came to us from the Treasury, and the wording of this provision was prepared in the Treasury. They said they would like to have that authority.

The CHAIRMAN. You did not have it before?

Mr. PINCHOT. The Treasury officials asked to have this particular passage which you have spoken of put in, and they prepared it themselves, thinking that is was necessary; and I should like to have it in; yes, sir. It makes it unnecessary for us to keep a certain amount of funds as unofficial.

The CHAIRMAN. Did the Treasury decide that you could not make those refunds?

Mr. PINCHOT. No, sir. We do that now by keeping a certain amount of money as unofficial, outside of our regular fund.

The CHAIRMAN. Did the Treasury hold that if that was deposited you could not use it for a refund?

Mr. PINCHOT. If it is put in the regular fund, we can not; no, sir; without this provision.

The CHAIRMAN. Of course there is no use in questioning the Treasury; but it says here in this act that "for a period of five years from the passage of this act" it "shall constitute a special fund, available until expended, as the Secretary of Agriculture may direct, for the protection, administration, improvement, and extension of the Federal forest reserves." I should think it was a pretty narrow decision. I should think that in your administration, if you received money that did not belong to you, you might pay it back.

Mr. PINCHOT. We have done it hitherto, Mr. Chairman, but we did it by that particular method.

Senator PERKINS. I would like to ask you one other question, Mr. Pinchot: How do you arrive at the value of the timber which you sell to buyers, the value of grazing lands which you lease to them for camping privileges or special water privileges or otherwise? In other words, timber in the Black Hills is of much greater value than it is in the Rocky Mountain Reserve?

Mr. PINCHOT. It is; very much.

Senator PERKINS. It is of greater value in some of the California reservations or forest reserves than it is farther north?

Mr. PINCHOT. Yes.

Senator PERKINS. How do you arrive at these values?

Mr. PINCHOT. We do it in two ways: In the first place, by finding out what timber is worth in that locality. We have expert lumbermen who are as good loggers, I think, as you will find—the best men we can possibly get. They go on the ground and interrogate people in the neighborhood, find out what the ruling price for timber is up there, and then find out what the logging is actually going to cost, and the result of it has been that most of our sales have been made at slightly higher prices than private individuals have sold timber for in the same neighborhood.

Senator PERKINS. Then, how about leased land for grazing purposes?

Mr. PINCHOT. We figure on the grazing with the idea of making a fee which is only nominal. It is at present, for the summer grazing season, from 20 to 35 cents for cattle and horses, and from 5 to 8 cents for sheep for the summer.

Senator MONEY. Can you not stop the sheep grazing?

Mr. PINCHOT. No, Senator; I do not think we can.

Senator MONEY. You will ruin the mountain sides if you do not.

Mr. PINCHOT. You will if you do not regulate it very carefully.

Senator MONEY. How do you regulate it?

Mr. PINCHOT. We do regulate it, with considerable results.

Senator MONEY. Effectively?

Mr. PINCHOT. Most effectively.

Senator MONEY. You do?

Mr. PINCHOT. Yes, sir; because a man who does not obey the regulations this year does not get in next year. We absolutely have control of that.

Senator PERKINS. Then, in leasing these lands, do you not enjoin upon them some protection to the forest from fires?

Mr. PINCHOT. We do.

Senator PERKINS. Do you hold them financially responsible?

Mr. PINCHOT. Every man who goes into lumbering is under bond, and it is part of his bond that if a fire occurs he must supply men to fight it; and we have found that both from the grazing men and from the timber-cutting men we have had a great deal of assistance in fighting fires. Our timber fees are about what timber is worth. We are getting up to $3.50 a thousand.

Senator LATIMER. I want to ask you there how you regulate the cutting? Do you allow them to cut timber above a certain measurement?

Mr. PINCHOT. No; we actually mark the trees that are to be cut; we select the trees and mark them. We brand them with a hammer with " U. S." on the back of it, and they cut only the trees that are marked. Then we have our scalers on the ground, and check scalers— a regular system like that of a lumber company—so that we see not only that they only take the trees that we mark, but that they pay for everything they take.

Senator LATIMER. And that is checked up in advance of the contract?

Mr. PINCHOT. No; we make the contract first. This money is deposited, covering, say, a fifth of the amount of timber that is to be sold. As soon as timber enough has been cut to meet the deposit, or about to meet the deposit, we notify the buyer, and he always has to have money on deposit with us covering the timber that is being cut, so that he never can get ahead of us. For grazing, the permit holder is required to pay in advance before his stock go into the territory.

Senator LATIMER. As to the timber that you cut there—I was trying to get at that point—what class of timber is it? How do you classify it?

Mr. PINCHOT. We generally say the timber above such and such a diameter limit. Roughly, in our instructions to our own officers, we will say timber above 12 inches in diameter 3 feet from the ground. Then the man who marks the timber is guided by that, but not absolutely. For instance, if he finds a tree that is going backward—that is, dead at the top and a little below the diameter limit—he will take that. If he finds a place where old trees are scant, and a 14-inch tree is needed to provide seed, he will leave it. The diameter limit is only a general guide.

Senator SIMMONS. Do you allow any tree to be cut that has not attained its full growth, unless it is in some way defective?

Mr. PINCHOT. No; we establish this diameter limit roughly, and then we stick to it, except for some such reason as you speak of.

Senator DOLLIVER. I did not notice any trees out in those Oregon woods that were 12 inches in diameter.

Mr. PINCHOT. Well, Senator, there are other places where the diameter limit would be 18 inches or 20 inches, depending on the character of the forest.

Senator DOLLIVER. Those trees seemed to be all about 5 or 6 feet through.

Mr. PINCHOT. Those ought to be cut.

Senator LATIMER. Do they utilize the tops of those trees pretty well?

Mr. PINCHOT. We require them to, absolutely.

Senator DOLLIVER. What do they do with them—burn them up?

Mr. PINCHOT. They cut all they can use under the circumstances, whatever it may be. It may be down to 5 inches or 4 inches for mine timbers, it may be down to 8 inches for ties, or it may be down to 10 or 12 inches for logs, just depending on the circumstances.

Senator PERKINS. I noticed last year in passing through the Kern River Forest Reserve, General Grant Park, that many of the trees have been cut down, and perhaps 40 or 50 feet of the butt length had been used for shakes or shingles, and the tops of the trees were left there as a menace, it seemed to me, from fire.

Mr. PINCHOT. Yes, sir; but, Senator, that cutting was not done in the forest reserve, I think.

Senator PERKINS. They claimed it was in the forest reserve. Some of it was just on the border, I think, and some of it was not, as you say. Possibly you are correct, that it was not on the forest reserve, but it was so near to it that I did not know the difference.

Mr. PINCHOT. We have never allowed anything of that kind.

Senator LATIMER. Another question: How do you handle this timber in the way of transportation? There is a good deal of forest reserve that has no railroad transportation.

Mr. PINCHOT. Yes. You see, we only sell timber on the stump.

Senator LATIMER. I know, but what do the manufacturers of the timber do?

Senator WARREN. They float it down streams at high water.

Senator PERKINS. They have flumes, Senator Latimer, 50 and 60 miles long, running from the Sacramento Valley and the San Quentin Valley into the Sierra Nevada Mountains, and of course the teamsters pull the timber to the sawmill.

Senator WARREN. Mr. Pinchot, about railroad ties: The pine in the Rocky Mountain country that they use for railroad ties is a species that usually does not grow much larger than that size, is it not?

Mr. PINCHOT. Yes, sir.

Senator WARREN. That is, it seems to be a growth specially designed for that use?

Mr. PINCHOT. Yes; the lodge-pole.

Senator WARREN. The lodge-pole pin. The diameter is perhaps 12 inches or such a matter, or 14 as the maximum?

Mr. PINCHOT. Yes; a great deal of it is just that size.

Senator WARREN. I asked that question in connection with the question asked by Mr. Simmons.

Mr. PINCHOT. Yes; oh, we have timber of all sizes, from 20 feet in diameter on the stump down to ripe timber at 10 or 12 inches, as Senator Warren was just saying.

Senator WARREN. In some places the lodge-pole pine is too small; it seems to die at a size less than that required for railroad ties, and it is only used for mine props and for fencing, etc.?

Mr. PINCHOT. Yes; exactly. We have an enormous area of dry timber.

Senator WARREN. You sell that at maturity, of course, the small sizes the same as the large?

Mr. PINCHOT. Yes; the same as the large.

One thing more: I was recently before the Senate Committee on Public Lands in connection with a bill to repeal the timber and stone act, and this same question that Senator Perkins has just raised about the forest-reserve fund came up. Those gentlemen were strongly of opinion that some kind of control by Congress over the expenditures of the forest service ought to be had; and I prepared this clause, which I will read in a moment, and submitted it to Senator Allison. I wanted to ask whether you thought it would be wise to put it in the bill or not. It reads like this:

The forest reserve special fund provided for in section 5 of the act approved February 1, 1905, entitled "An act providing for the transfer of forest reserves from the Department of the Interior to the Department of Agriculture," shall continue until otherwise provided by law——

It is now limited to five years.

But after June 30, 1908, it shall not be expended except in accordance with specific estimates of expenditures to be made from the said fund for the succeeding fiscal year, to be submitted by the Secretary of Agriculture with the estimates of appropriations in the annual Book of Estimates.

Senator WARREN. That is, this law we have just been quoting from?

The CHAIRMAN. It is in reference to that law, and you now propose to have that added here?

Mr. PINCHOT. I would suggest that if there is necessity that that might be added at the top of page 26 of the new bill. I would prefer the present condition for a year or two.

Senator WARREN. When you say the top——

Mr. PINCHOT. I mean the first paragraph, after line 4.

Senator PERKINS. I will say, Mr. Chairman, that I have been a member of the Committee on Appropriations for some ten or twelve years, and that is the policy that the Committee on Appropriations have always insisted upon—that that which is to be expended shall come to them in the form of the Book of Estimates.

The CHAIRMAN. What does Mr. Allison say to that?

Mr. PINCHOT. He thought that was good, sir. That is satisfactory to him.

The CHAIRMAN. That gives you the control of this fund until 1908?

Senator WARREN. He has it now.

The CHAIRMAN. I say it continues?

Senator WARREN. It does not extend it at all.

The CHAIRMAN. Now, suppose that was inserted, Mr. Pinchot, would it not change some of these later provisions? •

Mr. PINCHOT. No, sir.

The CHAIRMAN. It would not affect them?

Mr. PINCHOT. Not at all; no, sir. It simply provides that the Secretary shall state at the beginning of the year what it is proposed to do.

Senator PERKINS. Do you not think, Mr. Money, that that is proper to do?

Senator MONEY. Yes.

Senator PERKINS. We have always done that. Senator Warren is on the Committee on Appropriations.

Senator WARREN. The efforts have been all along to have just as nearly as possible everything estimated in the Book of Estimates, and, furthermore, to do away as much as possible with "slush funds," and have specific funds.

Senator PERKINS. I would like to move, Mr. Chairman, that that proviso be inserted on page 26, after the word "game," in line 4, making a new paragraph.

The CHAIRMAN. I think it is just as well to act on that now. Those in favor of inserting that amendment will say "aye."

(The amendment was unanimously adopted.)

The CHAIRMAN. Is there nothing further?

Mr. PINCHOT. Nothing further.

STATEMENT OF HON. JAMES WILSON—Resumed.

The CHAIRMAN. Now, Mr. Secretary, under the head of the Bureau of Chemistry there are, at the beginning, some changes of salary. Have you anything in particular to say about those?

Secretary WILSON. No; nothing in particular. Doctor Wiley is the Chief of the Bureau.

The CHAIRMAN. At the top of page 29, what is the use of changing the name of that office? Why not let it continue to read " one assistant property clerk," the same as the House had it?

Secretary WILSON. I think it is just as well. I do not think it makes any particular difference.

The CHAIRMAN. The other changes there are merely of amounts.

Senator WARREN. I notice that in your list of employees there, Doctor Galloway, there are some increases. We have just been working on the legislative and judicial bill and we want to go a little more slowly. For instance, if you raised a man from $720 instead of going to a thousand or nine hundred if you should perhaps go to eight hundred and forty and the next year raise it further, how would you feel about that?

Doctor GALLOWAY. All right; but we have not made any increases from $720 to $1,000.

Senator WARREN. I do not know that you have done that, but I was using that as a simile.

Doctor GALLOWAY. We practically follow the same policy there— that is, to promote from $720 to $840 and from $840 to $900 and from $900 to $1,000.

Secretary WILSON. That is a good idea. What page have you gotten to, Senator?

The CHAIRMAN. Page 30.

Secretary WILSON. Now, there is something to go out on page 32.

The CHAIRMAN. Page 32, "after notification," etc., at the top of the page.

Doctor GALLOWAY. We took that clause out simply to agree with the present law. Doctor Wiley asked that that be taken out to make the bill agree with the present law.

Senator LATIMER. I notice that you have changed the leave of absence to fifteen days. Why is that changed all the way through?

Secretary WILSON. I think that only continues for a year. I think we could not do it if it was not put in here.

Doctor GALLOWAY. That is simply to give to the field employees, Senator, leaves of absence for fifteen days.

Senator LATIMER. But I notice that you apply it all along here, all through here, to all the bureaus.

Doctor GALLOWAY. Some of the bureaus had it and some did not.

Senator WARREN. The difference has been practically that the ones in Washington got their leave, and those outside did not get any?

Secretary WILSON. Those outside did not.

Senator LATIMER. I thought they got thirty days.

Secretary WILSON. No, sir; they did not get anything. We want to give them fifteen days; but the field men would not get any leave.

Senator LATIMER. I mean the employees in the Bureau.

Secretary WILSON. Those in the field do not get any.

The CHAIRMAN. You ask for an additional clerk there.

Secretary WILSON. And for the increase of the money up to the estimates.

The CHAIRMAN. Yes. Now, on page 34, you want to strike out part of line 10, all of line 11, and part of line 12, reading, "and to secure, as far as may be, a change in the methods of supplying tobacco to foreign countries."

Senator WARREN. I judge that part below it to be an insertion.

Doctor GALLOWAY. That was an insertion made on the floor of the House.

Senator WARREN. That is a change.

Doctor GALLOWAY. It was simply to enable the Secretary to make certain investigations of tobacco markets in foreign countries.

Senator WARREN. How does that change suit you?

Doctor GALLOWAY. The change is agreeable to the Chief of the Bureau; that is all right.

The CHAIRMAN. You strike that out on account of the insertion below?

Doctor GALLOWAY. Yes, sir.

The CHAIRMAN. As it is embraced in that. Now, on page 35, that proviso is stricken out.

Doctor GALLOWAY. That proviso simply directed the Secretary to do some work in a particular county in New York, and did not authorize any additional money to do it with. It is one of those things that was added on the floor of the House.

Senator WARREN. It is unnecessary, is it not, and should be left out?

Doctor GALLOWAY. Yes, sir.

Secretary WILSON. It requires no law for a thing of that kind.

Senator WARREN. Which you do not want.

The CHAIRMAN. Now we come to the Bureau of Entomology. There are various changes there.

Secretary WILSON. We were speaking about that a while ago, in regard to the white fly.

The CHAIRMAN. Yes.

Secretary WILSON. I would like very much to have you increase that appropriation. I think the House gave that Bureau absolutely no increase at all.

The CHAIRMAN. As to the increase of clerks, there are several small items there asked for. Do you think they are necessary?

Secretary WILSON. Doctor Howard thinks they are necessary.

The CHAIRMAN. Very well; we will look those over. Now, while we are upon that, you have a good deal in lump sums, or that is the common impression; and much of that appropriation was made statutory a year ago. I would like to ask you whether or not more of those clerks can be put upon the statutory roll?

Doctor GALLOWAY. They are all there now, Senator. There are none on a lump-sum roll, except the recent appointees as a result of normal growth.

Secretary WILSON. There was a complete change last year.

Doctor GALLOWAY. And that is what these additions are for, in most cases. It is for the transfer from lump sums, in some cases—not all—simply to take care of the regular work. Now, if you wish to do so here, you can deduct that from the lump sum.

The CHAIRMAN. Have you not a good many employees now, under some name or other, that are paid from lump sums?

Doctor GALLOWAY. All scientific employees are paid in that way.

Senator WARREN. Did we not try to fix that last year?

Doctor GALLOWAY. It was fixed last year.

Secretary WILSON. Nothing but the scientists are paid in that way now. We have changed nobody from the statutory roll to the lump sum since that was done.

Doctor GALLOWAY. In the course of the year, as the work develops, if it becomes necessary to employ a clerk, the Secretary will get that clerk from the Civil Service Commission; but next year in his estimates he will include that clerk on the statutory list.

Senator WARREN. May I ask, Doctor Galloway, in relation to these several increases of clerks here in number, and so forth, and compensation—does that come largely from our leaving you short last year, or from increase in the work since?

Doctor GALLOWAY. From increase in the work since.

Senator WARREN. We gave you about what you required, did we not, last year?

Doctor GALLOWAY. Yes, sir; it is just the normal increase.

Senator WARREN. And this is the natural increase?

Doctor GALLOWAY. The natural increase.

Senator WARREN. Have you followed the practice here of raising salaries generally?

Doctor GALLOWAY. No, sir.

Senator WARREN. Or have you confined it to the meritorious cases?

Doctor GALLOWAY. Just to the particularly meritorious cases, where the record showed that the clerk deserved it.

The CHAIRMAN. Now, let me ask you another question—whether in any case in this bill, the case of clerks or appropriations, this bill as it came from the House goes beyond the estimate, or beyond what you asked for, in case we should grant it? I wish you would have it looked over and see if in any case the measure as it comes to us, or as we shape it, provided we put in what you ask for, goes beyond the estimate; and if it does, I want a supplementary estimate put in.

Secretary WILSON. I think we have not gone beyond the estimates in any case.

The CHAIRMAN. But you can have a clerk look that over.

Doctor GALLOWAY. I know what they are now, Senator. There are two or three cases, and we will give them to you.

Senator MONEY. Mr. Chairman, I suggest that there should be a memorandum of the reason for anything of that kind submitted to us.

Secretary WILSON. I think the House did that.

Senator MONEY. I want to be sure whether they have done it or not.

Senator WARREN. They have in some cases. Here is a case on page 28.

Secretary WILSON. We did not intend to bring you anything exceeding our estimates.

The CHAIRMAN. If you look them over, be sure that as we present the bill there is nothing beyond the estimates contained in it.

Secretary WILSON. But I wanted the estimates. I want the estimates that went first to the House committee to come to you also.

Senator WARREN. They do come.

The CHAIRMAN. We have those.

Secretary WILSON. I know you have.

Senator WARREN. There is also this $1,000 for forestry houses, as against $500. That you approve of, but that is also beyond the estimates.

The CHAIRMAN. We, of course, have not so ready a knowledge of the a s as you have. You can do that better than we can, or our clerk t il

Doctor GALLOWAY. That $3,500 in reference to the roads is a new thing.

Senator MONEY. What is that for?

Doctor GALLOWAY. The roads of the Department grounds.

The CHAIRMAN. You will see that an estimate is put in, giving the reasons, for anything that goes beyond the original estimate?

Doctor GALLOWAY. Yes, sir.

The CHAIRMAN. Now, the Bureau of Biological Survey, at the top of page 37—there are changes in clerks there. In all these cases where additional clerks are given I wish you would submit a statement covering every case.

Doctor GALLOWAY. Those statements are all in the estimates now, Senator. They are printed here in the estimates, and the reasons are given.

The CHAIRMAN. There is a reason given in every case, is there?

Doctor GALLOWAY. Yes, sir.

The CHAIRMAN. And you are asking for nothing beyond what is in the estimates?

Doctor GALLOWAY. For nothing beyond what is in the Book of Estimates.

The CHAIRMAN. Very well. Now, in the Division of Publications there are several changes.

Doctor GALLOWAY. It is the same case there.

Secretary WILSON. These are the original estimates, Senator.

The CHAIRMAN. Now, I have some memoranda on line 11, for example.

Secretary WILSON. Of what page?

The CHAIRMAN. Page 39, the Division of Publications, on line 11, "one editorial clerk, $1,600, omitted in estimate;" and on line 12, "one assistant in charge of illustrations, $2,000, omitted in estimate." I would like to have those covered, surely.

Secretary WILSON. I understood those were in the estimates. Look the book over and see; I think you will find them there. The Division of Publications has an increase of about $1,600 altogether for all these items.

Doctor GALLOWAY. Sixteen hundred and twenty dollars.

The CHAIRMAN. The Division of Publications have been very short of clerical help, and they have had a very small proportion of high-class clerks?

Secretary WILSON. Very small.

The CHAIRMAN. Now, in line 12, you change the name of one engraver.

Secretary WILSON. Yes, sir.

The CHAIRMAN. You change that to "assistant in charge of illustrations."

Secretary WILSON. Yes, sir.

The CHAIRMAN. What is the reason for that, except that it may sound a little sweeter?

Secretary WILSON. I think it is probably to bring him into harmony with other people in the class in which he is found.

The CHAIRMAN. Why will not "one engraver" do just as well?

Doctor GALLOWAY. Mr. Chairman, this employee is really not an engraver any more. He was formerly a wood engraver, and since wood engraving has gone out of style he has been put in charge of all of the illustrating and engraving work; and therefore, while he is still an engraver by profession, he is really not doing engraving work at this time and has not for several years.

Senator WARREN. Right there, it looks as if it was "one engraver, $1,800." It now reads, "one assistant in charge of illustration, $2,000."

Doctor GALLOWAY. There is a recommendation there for an increase.

Secretary WILSON. There is an increase of $1,000 in one place here and $600 in all these other things. That is what it amounts to.

Doctor GALLOWAY. Mr. Secretary, those are not in the estimates.

Secretary WILSON. They are not?

Doctor GALLOWAY. No, sir. There are a lot of other things in the estimates that are left out, but they have put those in.

The CHAIRMAN. You scratch out, in line 19, "one index clerk"— page 39.

Secretary WILSON. Yes, sir.

The CHAIRMAN. That is because you have added two above, I suppose?

Secretary WILSON. Two above; yes.

The CHAIRMAN. On page 40 there are a good many minor changes. That is quite an extensive revision there.

Doctor GALLOWAY. They are all minor, though, Senator. They do not involve any material increases in pay, and it is simply in connection with the reorganization of the division.

Senator WARREN. You have done away with a good many folders. Now, are you doing that work with more expensive men—clerks?

Doctor GALLOWAY. No, sir.

Secretary WILSON. A good many of those folders belong to that class of people that could only be promoted by taking the examination and successfully passing it; and they are getting out of the folding class.

Doctor GALLOWAY. And as the work increases more folders are required. They are brought in now from the civil service.

Secretary WILSON. I would like you to give a little more money to the Bureau of Statistics, to bring it up to the estimates. We want to change our statistical work a little bit, gradually. We want to put a little bit more money in the field.

Senator MONEY. That is right. Now, I would like to have an estimate prepared by you to put in here, a supplemental estimate for binding your bulletins up to No. 200, for instance; I do not know how many you have gotten out since. I put in a bill for that.

Doctor GALLOWAY. That is a very important thing.

Senator MONEY. I put in a separate bill for that, but the Committee on Printing said it would cost too much money. They informed me that to bind 6,000 volumes substantially would cost about $23,000—to print and bind 6,000 copies. It is too valuable a matter of information to send over the country in loose sheets. It ought to be preserved and kept together. They contain a most excellent fund of information.

Senator DOLLIVER. Is the proposition to bind them into one volume?

Senator MONEY. There are only 200. No; it will require about eight volumes.

Senator PERKINS. A resolution for that purpose was introduced in the Senate, you know. I thought they reported it favorably.

Senator MONEY. If they have, I have never heard it.

Senator PERKINS. We must do it.

Senator MONEY. I know the only reply I could get from that committee was the statement that it was too expensive.

Senator LATIMER. Do we not get the most valuable part of the bulletins in the Yearbook, Mr. Secretary?

Secretary WILSON. No; you do not get that. These are articles of a highly scientific character that go in there. You get them in little pamphlets, generally.

Doctor GALLOWAY. The farmers' bulletins ought to be filed together. They ought to be filed in libraries, where they are accessible as a unit, as a set, with an index. There are 200 of them now, and they represent pretty nearly all lines of agricultural and horticultural work.

Senator MONEY. Would you object to making a supplemental estimate for that, Mr. Secretary?

Secretary WILSON (after a consultation with Doctor Galloway). I will have to make inquiry as to whether we need that. My impression is that we can have that done with the authority we have now. I will try to inquire into it.

The CHAIRMAN. Now, Mr. Secretary, will you finish what you began to say about the Bureau of Statistics? That is on pages 42 and 43, I believe. I see you have made an addition there of $20,000.

Secretary WILSON. I would like to modify our present system of collecting statistics.

I would like to put a little more money in the field. I would like to have the State agent travel more, and give him money to pay his expenses and to travel. I think we could strengthen our reports from the States, if we did that. I would like to put a few hundred dollars more in each of those cotton States, and I should be disposed to let the clerks within the District of Columbia here become reduced—get along with fewer of them here and do more work in the field. To that end I would like to have the estimates here—some $20,000 more than is apropriated in this bill. The House did not put in anything additional under that item. The House took this view: That for the last six years that the Bureau had estimated the cotton crops, taking them and reducing them all to powers, it had come within seven-tenths of 1 per cent of the reports of the ginners; and the House members said: "Well, what is the use of appropriating anything more? If you come that close, as it is, what is the use of paying any more money for anything better?" That is the view the economists of the House committee take.

Senator LATIMER. Mr. Secretary, there is one point there that I want to mention, because I want the committee to think about it a little hereafter. I have been thinking a good deal about these reports from cotton. There are thirteen or fourteen States, I believe, in the South that grow cotton. If you have one man in each State to superintend all of the men who report from the different townships, located where you get reports from the weather, so as to take into account the rains that have fallen in any part of the State, and to keep you in telegraphic communication with the Department here, would not that be a great addition in getting accurate reports of the condition of crops every week?

Secretary WILSON. If we give a little bit more money to these State agents we can call on them to give us a little more information; we can work along that line; but we give them so very little now that they can not afford to do it.

Senator LATIMER. Will this $20,000 be sufficient?

Secretary WILSON. Yes; that is all we ought to have to work along the line of a modification of the cotton crop statistics.

Senator LATIMER. And that is what you want it for, largely?

Secretary WILSON. That is what I want it for—to strengthen the work done in the States and let it gradually become less and less in the District of Columbia.

Senator LATIMER. We made a fight last year to increase the appropriation so that you might have about $45,000 for that very purpose, so that you might give semimonthly reports. The idea was that the report of cotton, for instance, in the early part of the month, showing that a particular State was in a dry streak, for instance, and had not had rain for a certain time had to go on for a month's time, and sometimes that report as to the condition of the crop affected the price of cotton to the extent of a cent or a cent and a half a pound, and with a crop of four or five or six hundred million dollars it would amount to forty or fifty million dollars, probably, that a month's report might lose for the southern growers of cotton.

Secretary WILSON. It is in line with that suggestion that we would like to put a few more of our men in the States and get a little better and a little more extended and accurate information from the States.

The CHAIRMAN. Mr. Secretary, in view of everything that has occurred in relation to the Bureau of Statistics—all the criticisms, etc.—do you think it is wise to try to increase that appropriation?

Secretary WILSON. I am frank to say that that is the conclusion that the Committee on Agriculture in the House came to.

The CHAIRMAN. That it was not wise to do so?

Secretary WILSON. That is what they thought.

The CHAIRMAN. Very well.

Senator SIMMONS. Mr. Chairman, one of the chief reasons that there has been so much criticism about this cotton report, in my judgment, is that the Secretary has not had quite enough money to make his report as thorough as it ought to be in the interest of accuracy and in the interest of expedition. I think that if we can give him sufficient money to gather up this data quickly, probably some of these criticisms would disappear. Is there not something in that suggestion, Mr. Secretary?

Secretary WILSON. That is what I have been presenting to the committee. We think we could do that.

Senator DOLLIVER. My recollection is that there was never any criticism about the collection of the reports. The criticism was about the distribution of them.

Secretary WILSON. Yes—their premature distribution.

Senator SIMMONS. That has been the criticism with reference to the officials; but the criticism in the South of these reports has been that they are not gotten up as quickly and probably not quite as accurately as they might be; and that has been very largely due, I think, to the fact that the Secretary has not had quite enough money.

Secretary WILSON. And when all the cotton people who grow and handle and stem got together they had to admit that the best work done was done by the Bureau of Statistics of the Department of Agriculture.

The CHAIRMAN. Now, Mr. Secretary, you ask here for a large increase in the Bureau of Entomology.

Secretary WILSON. Yes.

The CHAIRMAN. You have not given any reason for that. Can you give one?

Secretary WILSON. There are reasons, sir.

Doctor GALLOWAY. The reasons are set forth in the estimates, Mr. Chairman.

It is because of the normal increase in the work, and it is specified there as to what those cases are.

Secretary WILSON. There are some letters here.

Doctor GALLOWAY. They are printed in the Book of Estimates, too.

Senator MONEY. Mr. Secretary, what was the difference between your estimate for statistical work and that allowed you by the House committee and by the House?

Secretary WILSON. Twenty thousand dollars.

Senator MONEY. How much did you ask for?

Secretary WILSON. Twenty thousand dollars additional.

Doctor GALLOWAY. And they did not give it.

Secretary WILSON. They did not give us anything.

The CHAIRMAN. We will meet again Friday morning and take up the free-seed matter for one thing, and I hope we will be able to go on and settle in executive session quite a portion of the bill.

(It was agreed that the committee should meet on Friday, and also on Saturday, if necessary; and the committee thereupon adjourned until Friday, May 11, 1906, at 10 o'clock a. m.)

DISTRIBUTION OF SEEDS.

COMMITTEE ON AGRICULTURE AND FORESTRY
OF THE UNITED STATES SENATE,
Washington, D. C., Friday, May 11, 1906.

The committee met at 10.30 o'clock a. m.

Present: Senators Proctor (chairman), Hansbrough, Dolliver, Perkins, Burnham, Money, Simmons, and Frazier.

The CHAIMAN. Well, gentlemen, I understand you have a delegation here representing the seedsmen. How much time do you want? We are some of us in favor of free seeds and some opposed. It is a pretty familiar topic, and I do not suppose anything that we hear will make much difference. We shall consider it. Still, we want to hear everybody fairly. How much time do you want?

Mr. LANDRETH. We were told we could have an hour and a half.

The CHAIRMAN. I do not want to shorten your time, but we hope that you will make your statement as concise as you possibly can. At the same time we wish to give everyone a hearing.

STATEMENT OF BURNETT LANDRETH, ESQ., OF BRISTOL, PA.

Mr. LANDRETH. Mr. Chairman, as chairman of this delegation, representing ten States, I will say that it is composed of wholesale seed merchants, retail seed merchants, seed farmers and other farmers, and two members of the grange organization, one the master of the National Grange and one the master of the Maryland Grange.

The object of our coming here to-day is to present our earnest protest against the continuance of free seed distribution, on the ground that it is in restraint of our trade and in restraint of our commerce. The Department of Agriculture distributes 40,000,000 packets of seeds annually. Now, all the seedsmen of the United States do not distribute more than 75,000,000 or 80,000,000 packets. Consequently, the Government distributes one-third, or more, of the seed that is distributed throughout the whole country.

We do not say that if the Government distribution was abolished, that we would sell 40,000,000 packets additional. We might sell

20,000,000 packets additional. These little packages, which are presented free by the Government and which are sold at 5 cents apiece by the retail dealers, represent a very large sum if 20,000,000 of them are so d.

We consider this distribution by the Government a restraint of trade. Congress is considering the regulation and restraint of objectionable trusts. Now, we claim that the Department of Agriculture, in distributing these 40,000,000 packages of seed, is conducting a trust in opposition to the interest of the seed trade in general, and we take it that before the Government investigates trusts in general they should abolish this seed trust. It is the Government which is conducting the seed trust, not the seedsmen. The Government is conducting an oppressive trust. It has the same effect, at least.

Then again, we object to the character of the seeds sent out. If they were of a better character, if they represented something that was an advantage to agriculture, it would be a different proposition; but they are the commonest things which our fathers and grandfathers had—squash, pumpkin, spinach. I need not name them. They are things which do not advance the interest of agriculture a particle. It is true the Department of Agriculture sends out some good things, twenty or thirty good things, some of them which have been obtained from China and Japan, as well as sugar beets and other things that might be mentioned, but not one good vegetable in the forty or fifty years that the seed distribution has been conducted; some garden vegetables, but not one good vegetable and not one good ornamental flower. They distribute some good agricultural seeds and some good plants and trees—peaches and plums and others things of that kind—but not one good article among the character of stuff comprising the 40,000,000 packages of seed.

Senator HANSBROUGH. Do you mean to say that the vegetable seeds sent out have been of an inferior quality?

Mr. LANDRETH. No, sir; I do not say that.

Senator HANSBROUGH. You said they were not good seed.

Mr. LANDRETH. No; I did not say that. I said they did not represent good things for the improvement and advancement of agriculture.

Senator HANSBROUGH. I supposed that was what you meant.

Mr. LANDRETH. We also say that these seeds are not wanted by the farming community. Who are the people that want them? They are the people who conduct back-yard gardens, not people who are engaged in agriculture. Not one of them is doing anything to advance agriculture. They want the seeds for the satisfaction of their palates, the same as they want a loaf of bread, and for nothing else.

Senator MONEY. What is the information on which you base your statement that the farmers do not want them?

Mr. LANDRETH. I am a seedsman, and am in correspondence with seedsmen all over the country, and farmers all over the country, and have a large list of buyers. My firm has been in the seed business for one hundred and twenty-two years continuously. It is the oldest seed house in America, and I ought to know.

Senator MONEY. You are just as badly mistaken about the farmers of Mississippi as though you had never been in the seed business a minute.

Senator HANSBROUGH. Yes; and also about the farmers of North Dakota.

Senator MONEY. Just as badly mistaken as though you had never heard of the subject, because they all seem to want the seed, and I can not get half enough.

Senator HANSBROUGH. Two-thirds of the letters I receive, beginning along about the 1st of February and continuing up to the end of the seed season, are requests for seed. I receive a great many every day.

Mr. LANDRETH. Are they from progressive farmers?

Senator HANSBROUGH. Oh, yes; all classes of farmers, and nearly all of them from farmers.

Mr. LANDRETH. It would take a mail bag of those seeds to do any good in supplying the ordinary kitchen. These little packages of seed sent out are merely flea-bites.

Senator PERKINS. If that is true, it does not injure your industry, does it? And then, in answer to the proposition of a trust, the Government does not grow these seeds; it purchases them from the growers.

Mr. LANDRETH. Yes; but the country merchant, who would otherwise lay in his stock of seeds from the seed dealers, is afraid to buy, because he does not know but what his locality will be deluged by the Congressional seeds and the seeds purchased by him will not be sold.

Senator SIMMONS. Does not that tend to show that the Congressional seeds, at least to a considerable extent, supply the demands of the farmer?

Mr. LANDRETH. No; it does not show that.

Senator SIMMONS. Otherwise the farmers would buy from the local dealer and the local dealer would provide a stock of seeds, would he not?

Mr. LANDRETH. As far as I can observe, the farmer is not the man who wants the seeds. It is the back-door gardener, the small cottage gardener, people who have not the interests of agriculture at heart, but who are looking for something to satisfy their palates. I take it that it is a waste of money and a restraint of trade.

Now, gentlemen, I have simply stated what the committee proposed to talk about, and I will introduce Mr. Henry B. Hathaway, from Rochester, N. Y., who is in the seed business.

STATEMENT OF HENRY B. HATHAWAY.

Mr. HATHAWAY. First, Mr. Chairman, I want to thank you gentlemen for the courtesy of this hearing, which, I believe, is somewhat unusual. As stated, I came from Rochester, otherwise frequently called the Flower City, the home of nurserymen and seedsmen and florists. The seed business is not my chosen profession, although I am in it pretty largely. The profession chose me. I was president and manager of a national bank for a great many years, which had the main deposits of seedsmen and nurserymen in our city. We had notably three seedsmen, old and well known as any in the United States, perhaps. One of them, after forty years of business, and two others, after about sixty years of business, having accumulated modest amounts, having supported hundreds of families, and having brought up their own families in their own business, were forced to fail.

They failed on the hands of the bank that I represented and got me into the seed business. They lay that failure mainly to the increased circulation or gift of free seeds, which has grown so widely from its original purpose.

As a boy on a farm some fifty years ago, my father was somewhat prominent as an old-line Whig. His Congressman sent him for several years, in the early stages of seed distribution, two or three packages of seeds, with a long request to state the date of planting, the soil, the general conditions, the care they had, the date of flowering, if they did flower, the date of perfection, the amount grown from the quantity of seed. The sheets containing these questions were religiously taken care of. They were put under the front page of the family Bible, were kept there until fall, when all the facts were ascertained, written down, signed, and sent back to the Department. Those were new and rare seeds. Many, if not all of them, were seeds that we, as farmers, knew nothing about and had never heard of. They were new varieties. That was a test of that soil, of that climate, and that part of the State.

Now, as you gentlemen know, the seeds are distributed by the 40,000,000 packages, and you also know, probably as well or better than I, how they are shipped, how they are dumped out on tables, and people frequently asked to help themselves, the 40,000,000 packages being about one-third of the entire number of packages of seeds used in the country. The country merchant or seed man dare not order, because he does not know how many Congressional seeds will come to that immediate town or whom they will come to, and so in many cases the country merchant waits until so late, and then, perhaps, from a change of Congressman or something of that kind the Congressional distribution is omitted, and so I honestly believe that the Government distribution of seeds decreases rather than increases the number of vegetables grown in the United States.

Senator MONEY. Let me ask you a question right there. What is the source of your information that these seeds are dumped on tables and everybody asked to come and help himself?

Mr. HATHAWAY. I have seen them.

Senator MONEY. That is not a general thing. I have never seen it. The fact is, I never send out any seeds except as special requests come. I distribute mine among the Representatives from my State, and they send them out addressed to individuals. The addresses are written on slips of paper and then pasted onto the packages. I have never known an instance where the Department delivered in the way you speak of—have never known an instance of that kind in all the time I have been here.

Mr. HATHAWAY. I suppose the theory of distribution is that these packages shall be sent separately to individuals.

Senator MONEY. And that is the practice.

Mr. HATHAWAY. I suppose it is generally the practice. What I said in regard to that is based on the fact that a member of Congress from our district, in western New York, the year before, and, I suppose, in the hope of renomination, made some arrangement by which he distributed widely through his own district his own quota of seeds. He also obtained half of some other Congressman's quota of seeds and sent that into the district.

Senator MONEY. That is quite common.

Mr. HATHAWAY. Several mail bags of them were dumped on a table placed there for that purpose in this gentleman's place of business, and these I saw, and people were freely invited to help themselves. A good many of them were taken, but I should say 3 or 4 or 5 bushels of them were never taken at all.

Senator MONEY. Now, you may just consider that an exception to the rule, and not the rule. The rule is the other way.

Mr. HATHAWAY. What I have stated will be borne out not by those who are here in Washington engaged in the transaction of the public business, but those of us who are around among the farmers, in farming communities, everywhere and all the time. We know the exceptions.

Senator MONEY. I know the rule.

The CHAIRMAN. Did you give the percentage of the total seed consumption of the country that you thought was distributed by Congress? I understood you to say something about one-third.

Mr. HATHAWAY. The first speaker said that the seedsmen sold 70,000,000 and odd, and that the Government distributes 40,000,000 packages free. I believe that is the fact.

Mr. LANDRETH. Yes. Now, with your permission, I will introduce ex-Governor Nathan J. Bachelder, of Concord, N. H., master of the National Grange, Patrons of Husbandry.

STATEMENT OF EX-GOVERNOR NATHAN J. BACHELDER.

' Mr. BACHELDER. Mr. Chairman and members of the committee, I am here representing the National Grange, a farmers' organization of about 800,000 members, represented in 30 States. A year ago last November, at the annual session of the National Grange, held at Portland, Oreg., this question was under discussion. It was quite fully considered, and at the close of the discussion the following action was unanimously taken:

We are unanimous in the conclusion that while the Agricultural Department at Washington should exert due diligence in its research for new food, forage, and other plants, and while there is something that can and perhaps should be done through the exchange of seeds, we can not conclude otherwise than that the general and free distribution of the many common kinds and varieties of garden and field seeds by the Department is without benefit in any important sense, and should be abandoned.

That is the resolution taken by the National Grange, as I said, after quite a full discussion of the matter. It is not necessary for me to take your time further.

Senator SIMMONS. What is the membership of that grange? Is it largely composed of farmers?

Mr. BACHELDER. Farmers.

Senator SIMMONS. Or business men?

Mr. BACHELDER. Farmers.

The CHAIRMAN. Almost exclusively farmers?

Senator MONEY. And about what is the membership?

Mr. BACHELDER. About 800,000.

Senator SIMMONS. How many delegates were present when you passed this resolution?

Mr. BACHELDER. Two delegates from each State. There were more present, but the action was taken by two delegates from each State.

Senator FRAZIER. How many States were represented?

Mr. BACHELDER. I think 27 States.

The CHAIRMAN. Does this organization exist in nearly every State?

Mr. BACHELDER. It exists in about 30 States. The organization in New York numbers about 75,000 members.

The CHAIRMAN. Is it extending in other States? Is it growing?

Mr. BACHELDER. It is growing very rapidly. In the past eight years it has increased 87 per cent in membership.

Senator PERKINS. The first speaker made the point that the Government was infringing upon private rights and private interests by going into the seed business. Do you think it does so in that respect any more than it does in others? This, of course, is apart from the question of policy or expediency. You have in your State a navy-yard, and you are asking appropriations to do work in that navy-yard, repairing ships and other work of that kind. Our friend from Rochester has printing offices there. Then, on the same line of reasoning, we might say that the printing of agricultural reports and other reports by the Government is infringing upon the rights of the people and their interests. A man who builds a dredge to do work for the Government——

Senator MONEY. Or makes rifles.

Senator PERKINS. I only wanted to ask you your views on that question. You will remember that the first speaker emphasized that fact.

Mr. BACHELDER. My opinion is that the opposition of this organization is based upon the fact that there is no benefit to agriculture that comes from it, no aid to the promotion of agriculture.

Senator PERKINS. That question alone is, I think, the question that the committee out to consider.

Mr. BACHELDER. We find that most of these seeds can be purchased in country stores in all pa s of the country.

Senator PERKINS. Would you not favor the purchasing or providing by the Department of Agriculture, either by importation from abroad or cultivation at home, of rare seeds and new seeds of economic value, improvements in the cotton plant and in the tobacco plant, and things of that kind?

Mr. BACHELDER. I am of the opinion that that work should be done by the experiment stations, and that the results obtained by them should be given to the farmers in the different States.

Senator PERKINS. You think better results would come from it in the geographical locality in which it is situated?

Mr. BACHELDER. I think so.

Senator SIMMONS. Governor, are you a farmer?

Mr. BACHELDER. Yes. In order to enforce what I have said in regard to these seeds not being of any benefit to the promotion of agriculture, I will just take the time for a moment to say that on my way to the train, in coming here, I met a friend of mine who had just received a package of seed from the Government, and when I remarked to him that I expected to appear before this committee he said: "I would like to have you take that package and ask the committee what benefit the committee thinks comes to the promotion of agriculture from the distribution of those seeds." Now, I find here a package of Stone tomato seed, a package of Big Boston lettuce, a package of moss curled parsley, a package of round yellow Danvers onions, and a package of scarlet turnip white-topped radish.

I question if there is any benefit to agriculture from the distribution of such seeds.

Senator PERKINS. They are not California seeds. We put up large quantities of seeds, and my constituents are complaining that the Government did not buy all the seeds in California, but went to Rochester. It is very hard to satisfy all our constituents. [Laughter.]

Mr. LANDRETH. Mr. Chairman and gentlemen, I wish to introduce Mr. John Fottler, jr., of Boston, Mass.

STATEMENT OF MR. JOHN FOTTLER, JR., OF BOSTON, MASS.

Mr. FOTTLER. Mr. Chairman and gentlemen, I wish to present, as my quota to this entertainment, a matter entirely different from what has been presented by the gentlemen here, and I will try to be brief. 1 speak with a little pride for my line of business. I have been a seedsman for forty-six years. That is longer than the average life of man. I should like to stay here a little longer and endeavor to keep an honorable name, and when I go away from the business I should like to leave an honorable name behind me, the same as I believe every other honorable and honest seedsman would like to do.

Now, there seems to be an impression that arose from a pretty hot argument in the House of Representatives a little while ago. I wish to read six lines from that argument:

> It is said that the seed dealers are opposed to it. That is very sad, and I say they are behind the instigating of these newspaper articles, opposing this measure, and I am going to make the broad assertion that some of the greatest commercial thieves and scoundrels in this country are among the seedsmen, and I will prove the truth of my assertion.

Senator FRAZIER. From whom do you quote?

Mr. FOTTLER. The Hon. South Trimble, of Kentucky.

Senator MONEY. We never take notice of language used in the other House. [Laughter.]

Mr. FOTTLER. I have been taken for a Kentucky colonel myself, so I am willing to excuse intemperate language.

Now, gentlemen, this whole subject seems to me to resolve itself into two problems. The first is that the farmer needs certain education that he gets from the receiving of these seeds. The second is that he can not buy from dealers such good seed as the Government sends him free of charge. Those seem to be the two propositions of the gentlemen who favor the distribution of these seeds.

I will not undertake to go into the question of the education of the farmer, but I will read one letter to back up the second assertion. When this argument was first started, I wrote President Roosevelt a letter in behalf of the seed trade of my State, asking his attention to the subject. I knew he was a good sportsman, and I thought he was a lover of fair play, so I took it upon myself to write him a personal letter. He referred my letter to Secretary Wilson. Now, I have great respect for Secretary Wilson and all the officers under him, and I am not here to criticise unduly anything that may have been done by our good and honest servants in the Department. But in reply Secretary Wilson wrote this letter to the President:

DEPARTMENT OF AGRICULTURE,
OFFICE OF THE SECRETARY,
Washington, D. C., March 5, 1906.

The PRESIDENT:

I have received by reference from the White House, a letter to you from the Schlegel & Fottler Company, 26 South Market street, Boston, Mass., in which is inclosed a document purporting to be signed by all the seed dealers in Boston protesting against the free distribution of seed by this Department under the appropriation made therefor.

This document induces me to say one or two things.

First, I have asked Congress to stop the distribution of seeds other than new, rare, and valuable varieties. Secondly, the pressure for seeds comes from the people because they can not buy from seedsmen generally as good seeds as this Department sends out. The "laboring oar" is in the hands of the seedsmen; let them take the care that we take in the growing and testing of seeds, and the people will be satisfied to buy from them.

Very respectfully,   JAMES WILSON, *Secretary.*

I know I am not telling you gentlemen anything new when I read that.

Senator DOLLIVER. Do you sell to the farmers direct?

Mr. FOTTLER. We sell to the farmers direct all over the country.

Senator DOLLIVER. I think the Secretary had in mind the fact that the same old box of seeds is set out in front of the grocery store for about ten years in succession.

Mr. FOTTLER. The sale of seeds by the country merchant is the thing that this free distribution of seeds by the Government interferes with more than anything else. Personally, this might not interfere with our seeds so very much, but it is the principle we are standing up for.

Senator HANSBROUGH. How does the quality of the seeds distributed by the seedsmen compare with the quality of seeds distributed by the Government?

Mr. FOTTLER. I am coming to that in a moment. The Department has to buy from the seed trade probably nine-tenths of all the seeds they have ever sent out in the last forty years.

Senator HANSBROUGH. Is the Government seed as good as that which is distributed by the seedsmen?

Mr. FOTTLER. I am not going to say that it is not as good. I am not around calling out "stale fish," but I want to say that when the Department pays, in California, 17 cents a pound for onion seeds, and we seedsmen pay from 40 to 50 cents a pound, either we are very stupid or the Department is very keen in its business transactions. I can not say that the Department does not get just as good seed for 17 cents as we do for 50, but I leave it for the committee to judge whether that is a natural result.

I want to go on to the question of what has arisen from an act of Congress that was promulgated some little time ago, which authorized and, in fact, demanded that the officers of the Department should put out a dragnet and collect samples, particularly of grasses and clovers, and make an examination of them and publish to the world the result. Now, that is one thing that perhaps may not interest the committee, but I think it should, from the fact that some one has said that the seedsmen are scoundrels and thieves, and some one has proposed to prove it. I do not know that I want to leave that to you, gentlemen, but I want to make this statement, so that you may understand just what happened.

In the first place, they asked us for samples, and we sent them, believing that we were sending the best we could. Then they sent their agents around and got a half peck, or 4 pounds, samples which they sent to the Department to examine microscopically. The result of that was that without notice to us, or without our being aware of the thing we were led into, a great many houses and men were published broadcast throughout the country, and the papers took it up, and the statement made that they were manifestly dishonest. Now, when a body of men constitute themselves judge and jury and executioners without a hearing to the culprit some damage is sure to come. I will give you one instance. Mr. Gregory, of Marblehead, a man as honest as the day is long, was asked for a sample of orchard-grass seed. He was asked for 4 pounds of it, and he did not have it. He had not had any for a long time. He had not had any call for it; but when somebody sent to him and asked him for 4 pounds of it he sent to a dealer to get it, and having obtained it from some one else in order to fill this order for 4 pounds, he sent it on, and it was sent to the Department. It turned out that somebody had mixed it, and it grew mixed, and Mr. Gregory's name was published. You see that was a great injustice to a man who had simply tried to do the right thing without any fault on his part.

Senator DOLLIVER. He might have avoided that by stating that he was not dealing in that grass seed.

Mr. FOTTLER. I know; but, gentlemen, understand that a man likes to fill his orders. Some one ordered half a peck, or 4 pounds, of orchard-grass seed from him, and he sent to some one, in Boston, I presume, and got it. He may have got it from us. I do not know. Our own sample was a little better than his, but at any rate he sent this package, and that was all he had in his shop of that orchard-grass seed, and in trying to accommodate some customer back in Vermont who wanted it for the Government this gross injustice was done to poor Mr. Gregory. The mere statement of this case and the history of this sample that he obtained, as he supposed, to accommodate a customer shows the injustice that was done him.

Senator FRAZIER. It also shows that the seed that was tested was very defective.

Mr. FOTTLER. It does seem so.

Senator DOLLIVER. It does not take a jury to settle the difference between clover seed and something else.

Mr. FOTTLER. This was orchard grass. The sample contained seed that no ordinary seedsman can detect. There are not three seedsmen in this country who are used to a microscopical examination of seeds. It requires a special education, such as Doctor Galloway has, and Mr. Pieters, and but very few men in this country. I can name half a dozen varieties of the same species of seed that even they can not tell without a microscopical examination. They are so close in their resemblance that the ordinary seedsman can not tell, and I will back that statement up by a letter from Mr. Pieters. Then another man, Mr. Grossman, of Petersburg, Va., was posted, and his seed contained 1¼ per cent of some other clover seed. That was very unjust, because absolutely pure clover seed is out of the question. We very rarely see such a thing. Our own house was posted because we sent a sample of orchard seed that contained 6.2 per cent of another common grass, almost exactly similar in appearance.

Senator Money. You are simply impeaching the methods of the Department. You are not addressing yourself to the question of the distribution of seeds at all.

Mr. Fottler. I understand that.

Senator Money. You want to convict the Department.

Mr. Fottler. I thought it might be well for me to show that we would like to come before the Senate with clean hands, and I thought if some one in the Senate should propose to follow the course of the gentleman in the House we should like to have them know the facts.

Senator Money. I will vouch for the Senate that it will not do it.

Senator Dolliver. You will admit, I suppose, that there are seedsmen——

Mr. Fottler. I can not tell, because I have some documents here from the Department that leave me in doubt as to whether there are any dishonest seedsmen. Mr. Pieters himself says it is a question. I want simply to say that in our own case we have been published in the Boston Herald and in some other papers, and the result has been some serious lawsuits. We brought suit against the Herald. We can not allow our name to go out to the public in that way. As a result, we are defending ourselves.

I read the other day a Government pamphlet, Farmers' Bulletin No. 111, by A. J. Pieters, a very fine gentleman. This testimony was published before. The edict went forth from Congress to try and see what they could find against us, what holes there were in our coats. This bulletin was published in 1900, and I will read one brief extract:

RELIABLE SEEDSMEN AND THE DEMAND FOR CHEAP SEED.

It is hardly necessary to insist that some seed dealers are more reliable than others. There are plenty of honest seedsmen in the United States, and these aim to treat a customer fairly, but many of these firms have not an adequate knowledge of grass and forage-pant seeds, and are almost as liable to error as the purchaser himself.

The means of identification is so difficult. I have been in business a long time, and I can not tell the difference between Canadian blue grass and Kentucky blue grass with my eye, when they are mixed, and I doubt if there are three men in the country who are not microscopists that can tell. He says:

A firm that can be depended upon in the sale of grasses and clovers must not only be honest, but must have a special knowledge of the seeds it sells. Such firms usually offer their customers a fancy article and urge them to buy it in preference to the cheaper grades, but the latter must be handled because of the demand for them.

At a meeting of seedsmen one of the number said that he had been advised to continue offering high-grade seeds, although the demand did not seem to justify it, and these grades were not profitable. The reason given to him was that it would help his reputation, and that so long as people were foolish enough to buy low grades and tailings his profits would come from the sale of these low grades. It is true that seedsmen find less profit in the high grades than they do in the cheaper ones, and no dealer can afford to confine his trade to the former. He must keep what his customers demand. But how much more profitable for the customer to buy the high-grade seeds.

Well, now, this is simply a question of the conditions with which we are confronted. Nature does not produce seeds in purity in any case. It never was known, and we are in a box to know what to do when we are offered certain grades of grass seed. As Mr. Gregory said, " Don't stir it up, because the next thing they will pass a law to send us to State prison," and they would come pretty near doing it. I want simply to say that the reputable seedsmen are in the majority, and they wish to have it understood that they care for their reputation, and that they do the very best they can for themselves and their customers in handling what they send out.

Senator PERKINS. I do not think the committee desires to impeach the integrity or the honesty and good faith of the seedsmen. The question for us to determine is, Is it policy, is it expedient for the Government to continue what it is doing through these different Departments, among them the Agricultural Department? That Department issues these bulletins upon cheese making, butter making, bee raising, hop raising, horticulture, and viticulture, and in connection with that the Department distributes to our constituents in the different States and Territories certain seeds. The simple question, it seems to me, is, Is it policy for the Government to continue that course which it has been proceeding in for the past forty years? Is this committee to report against it?

Mr. FOTTLER. Every seedsman who is here to-day feels that this committee and the entire Senate thoroughly understand the position of the seedsmen; but after being roasted so badly in the House as to our reputation, we thought this committee might not object if we devoted five minutes simply to saying that we could not let that go by default.

Senator PERKINS. The only question we want to determine is, is it policy for us to continue in doing what we have been doing heretofore?

Mr. FOTTLER. I understand that is the main question.

Senator PERKINS. I am decidedly in favor of certain kinds of seeds being distributed.

Mr. FOTTLER. I ought to say one thing more. I have letters here from the Department of Agriculture officials, from Doctor Galloway, and I think Doctor Galloway really regrets that the thing went so far in this dragnet business. I have his letter here, and he says that he would be very glad to modify their views about this, that absolute purity can not be expected, and that he thinks hereafter we will not have any trouble over that; but the mischief has been done. Of course I feel a little sore on this thing, to have my friends come in and say, " Well, you finally got it, didn't you? You are caught all right. This is nice business, isn't it, for you men to get caught?" And it unfortunately happened that in the same paper there was a story, a whole column, about a drug firm being fined $200 for selling adulterated drugs. Then it follows right along, "Adulterated seeds."

Senator PERKINS. Speaking of your friend who abused you, which you seem very sensitive about, I will tell you my experience. I wanted some Kentucky blue grass, and I sent to Kentucky for a ton of it and got it, and when it came up half of it was red clover. Alfalfa seed is the same way.

Mr. FOTTLER. The appearance of the two is vastly different, of course, and seedsmen——

Senator PERKINS. Oh, it did not reflect pa   a   on that seedsman. He bought it, and it was represented to him as being all right.

Mr. FOTTLER. Had it come up partly Canadian blue grass that

might have been expected, because the two species are almost identical in the appearance of the seeds, and that mistake could have been made very easily; but to have red clover come up, that was inexcusable. No seedsman should make that mistake.

Mr. LANDRETH. Mr. Chairman, I will next introduce Mr. Patrick O'Mara, of Peter Henderson & Co., New York.

STATEMENT OF PATRICK O'MARA.

Mr. O'MARA. Mr. Chairman and gentlemen of the committee, as I understand from the Senator from California [Mr. Perkins], the real question before you is whether or not it is good policy for the Congress of the United States to continue this free distribution of seeds. We are-here to protest against it and to lay before you such reasons as we can conjure up and such reasons as we believe to be true and legitimate against the further continuance of it.

I was struck by a remark of the Senator from California about hanging a man before they tried him. In the part of the country that I came from there used to be a man known as Jack the Stringer, a judge, of whom it was said that he hanged a man first and then tried him afterwards. It seems to me that seedsmen are somewhat in the position of the people who came before that judge.

Now, with the permission of the committee, I am going to refer briefly to the time when the free distribution of seeds first began. As I understand the law, the Congress of the United States appropriated $1,000 for the purchase of new, rare, and valuable seeds, to be distributed throughout the United States, for the purpose of increasing the output of agriculture. To the best of my knowledge and belief no seedsman protested against that and no farmer protested against it. We have here to-day both seedsmen and farmers protesting against the present method of carrying out the original intent of that act. I noticed in the debate in the House—which, I understand, Senators do not notice, but which I will take the liberty to allude to—that one of the founders of our country, the late Thomas Jefferson, is lauded for going into Italy and stealing some rice, which he brought in the pockets of his coat, first into France and from France into the United States, as a result of which the rice output of South Carolina was materially increased, and remains to the present time at a standard that it would not have been without the very praiseworthy act of the late President Jefferson.

In that connection I wish to say that with all the wisdom of Thomas Jefferson I have yet to find that he advocated the distribution of the common rice of South Carolina to other parts of the country. I respectfully submit that at the present time the free distribution of common garden seeds is on a plane of that kind—that is, that you are distributing what may increase the output of agriculture, it is true, because every seed that is sown and that reaches maturity adds to the wealth of the country to that extent, but I submit that that is not in line with the original intent of the act. Now, at the present time the seedsmen and agriculturists of the United States do not protest against, but in fact they welcome every attempt made to introduce into the country from any source whatever new and improved varieties of seeds, plants, and bulbs. But what we do protest against,

I repeat, is the free distribution of the ordinary varieties of vegetable seeds and flower seeds.

Senator FRAZIER. Why do you protest against that? Let us have the reasons why you do that.

Mr. O'MARA. As I view it, Senator, it is not a proper function of the Government to supply ordinary articles of commerce to the citizens of the United States. Admitting that principle, I fail to see where you can readily stop. If you supply the farmer with seeds because he wants them, and I want whisky, I do not see why I am not just as much entitled to my daily or weekly or monthly or yearly quota of whisky as the farmer is to his seeds or any other article that might be named. That is the layman's way of understanding it and the layman's comprehension of it.

Now, gentlemen, to pursue that just a little further: As I understand it, after the law went into effect, when the Commissioner (I believe it was first the Commissioner of Patents) expended that money as wisely as he could, to get new varieties of vegetable seeds or whatever they were, he found the demand from outside everywhere was greater than he could supply. The appropriation was increased and increased and increased, and that appropriation was used, not for the original purpose of the act—to distribute these seeds so that the recipient of them should get what he wanted and what he requested—but such as Congress saw fit to send to him, perhaps because they could not find enough of the new, rare, and valuable varieties.

I respectfully submit that when the Commissioner of Patents, and later the Commissioner of Agriculture, found that he could not spend, in accordance with the law, the amount of money placed at his disposal for the purchase of these new, rare, and valuable seeds, he should have said so, and should have refrained from going into the market and doing what it is doing, and, as I understand it, as the Congress of the United States at the present time has its finger on the index and can move it where it pleases, I respectfully submit that it is for the Congress of the United States to move that index back to the principle of right, which was involved in the original act. That is what we contend for.

Now, if you will pardon me just a moment, it may not be germane to the discussion, but I am going to say this: As I understand it, Congress bases its action principally upon the demand made by the constituents of its members. It is for you, gentlemen, as lawmakers, to determine whether that is right or not. We common florists do not profess to know. Although I have my own ideas, I am not bold enough to put them before you. You are better judges of that than I am. As I said before, admitting the right of the citizen to demand seeds, I fail to see where you can prohibit his right to demand anything else and still stand squarely upon the question of right.

Senator PERKINS. As you are discussing this so very intelligently, let me suggest one thought to you. Farmers say that every other industry of the country is fostered and protected and assisted by the Government except that of agriculture and the horticultural and viticultural interests, and they claim that this distribution of seeds is an indication on the part of the General Government that they recognize the great industry of agriculture and are willing to foster it and assist it and bring the farmers in touch with the Department. That is one line of argument briefly.

Mr. O'MARA. As against that we place the testimony of all the seedsmen of the United States, who are in touch with the entire agricultural community; as against that we place the testimony of all the agricultural and horticultural papers of the United States. Not one at the present time that I know of has raised its voice in favor of the continuance of the system. As against that we place still further the National Grange of the United States, represented here to-day, and the Maryland Grange, represented in the person of the master of that grange. We place as against that claim the entire interested part of the United States, as far as they can be represented by representatives, by papers, or by their voice in the public press. Now, I was going just one step further——

Senator DOLLIVER. Who is it, then, that is making this demand? The members of the House are as smart as chain lightning to tell what the public demand.

Mr. O'MARA. I will speak for my own district, Senators, if you please. That may be an indication. I live in Jersey City, N. J. Hudson County. was at one time the garden spot of New York and produced a large quantity of the vegetables required. Now, the last distribution of garden seeds there was distributed through a political organization.

Senator MONEY. What political organization?

Mr. O'MARA. The Samuel D. Dickinson Association; a political organization in Jersey City.

Senator MONEY. What is it, Democratic or Republican?

Mr. O'MARA. We had two Republican representatives from that county at that time, which, of course, would naturally account for the manner of distribution. I was going to say that I do not know how many people in Hudson County asked for the seeds. I am certain there are some. If you should offer to give away jackstraws somebody would ask for them. It is human nature to want to get something for nothing, so that any demand from constituents for something that cost them nothing I think should not be weighed in the balance at all.

Senator DOLLIVER. What is one of those little papers of seeds worth?

Mr. O'MARA. As nearly as we can figure it out, they are worth about 5 cents apiece. The total output to the Government, I think, is about a cent and a quarter per package, to which should be added the cost of distribution.

Senator FRAZIER. What do the seedsmen sell them for?

Mr. O'MARA. Five cents apiece. The cent and a quarter a package is the original cost to the Government, and then there is the cost of distribution—the postage and all that. All that is not counted in. Then there is rent, light, and all the other things of that kind are not counted in, which the seedsmen of necessity must count in. I was going on to say that the Congressman from Hudson County, who is not there now, I am sorry to say, because he was a good Democrat. That Congressman distributed seeds through the public schools in Jersey City, and Mr. Forbes, of Peter Henderson & Co., has some boys going to the public schools, and he was astonished one day when his boys came home with a package of seeds, and they were chewing the parsley seeds. That was the use to which the seeds went.

That was rubbing it in. Now, gentlemen, I might pursue this line, but you know it all just as well as I do. I might go on in other lines and take up all your time. I simply want to say in conclusion that in protesting against the free distribution of seeds by the Government, we protest against it as not being of value to agriculture or to the country at large in proportion to the expenditure. We protest against it as being wrong in principle. We do not protest against the free distribution of rare seed; we do not protest against the dissemination of literature; we do not protest against any line of investigation by the Department; even though it touches the seedsmen. We do not claim to be angels with wings.

Senator DOLLIVER. Would you be satisfied if we made provision that these seeds should be distributed upon the request of individuals, for individual distribution?

Mr. O'MARA. Personally, I should not, sir. Personally, I do not see any possible reason for the distribution of the common varieties of garden seeds.

Senator DOLLIVER. If a farmer should write to a Representative, asking him to send him garden seeds, that is a habit that has been growing for forty years——

Mr. O'MARA. Personally, I am opposed to that.

Senator PERKINS. As I understand it, you recommend the introduction of rare and valuable seeds.

Mr. O'MARA. Take, for instance, the work the Department is doing in cotton, tobacco. Take the work the Department is doing in lettuce at the present time. I had the pleasure of seeing something that they are doing in that regard.

Senator PERKINS. And in viticulture and horticulture.

Mr. O'MARA. In viticulture and horticulture, I should say they should continue their work on the new varieties, wherever they can get them, and propagate them and distribute them through the experiment stations. They are splendid vehicles of distribution.

Senator PERKINS. You know what Burbank has done with grass seed, you know what he has done with the cactus——

Mr. O'MARA. That is a dangerous subject for me, sir.

Senator PERKINS. You know what he is cultivating on arid lands and on very moist lands. Would you have the Department continue such things? I am only asking your opinion.

Mr. O'MARA. Yes, Senator.

Senator PERKINS. I only ask you on these lines to what extent you would go, and I should like to have you elaborate it.

Mr. O'MARA. I would say this: I believe at the present time there is no law in the United States that allows the Government of the United States to purchase a new variety.

Senator PERKINS. Is there any prohibition of that?

Mr. O'MARA. There is no prohibition so far as I know, but I do know that men have sought to place new varieties with the United States Government, to have it buy them, and the Department has told them that it is not within the law for them to do it.

Senator PERKINS. That is new to me.

Mr. O'MARA. If they have $75,000 for the distribution of new, rare, or valuable varieties——

The CHAIRMAN. I think you are mistaken in your idea about that. I think they have authority to purchase.

Mr. O'MARA. I know the reply which has been made by the Department to offers that have been made to the Department.

Senator MONEY. The Department has done a great deal of work in the discovery and introduction of foreign varieties of seeds, plants, bulbs, and things of that sort.

Senator PERKINS. The question I wish to ask was as to the extent to which you would go in that direction.

Mr. O'MARA. I would place at the disposal of the Department of Agriculture every dollar necessary; I would not care how much it is. I know that it can not exceed the reasonable credit of the United States. I would place at the disposal of the Agricultural Department every dollar that they would ask——

Senator PERKINS. What amount would you approximate?

Mr. O'MARA. I would say $100,000 the first year—I believe the amount this year is between $70,000 and $75,000, as it comes before the Senate—for the distribution of new, rare, and valuable seeds. I say give them a hundred thousand dollars, or give them $150,000. I would double the amount and give them $150,000 for the purchase of new, rare, and valuable varieties of seeds, plants, and so forth.

Senator PERKINS. For distribution through the experiment stations?

Mr. O'MARA. Through the experiment stations, so that they would reach the people in that way. There are new varieties constantly cropping up. I have in mind one gentleman who has a new raspberry, and one or two others, who have offered them to the Department of Agriculture, and the reply was that they were not able to purchase, and I took it for granted that the law prohibited them from doing it. I say, let the Department get the new things.

I had the pleasure of visiting Mr. Burbank's place last summer, and I saw that thornless cactus (I can not recall the particular name of it). I say that is a perfectly legitimate work, and the kind of work that the Department ought to do. In that particular instance I do not think they were on the right track, but I do not quarrel with them about that, because the principle is right. I say wherever there is a man like that that the Department can use in the pursuit of knowledge, for distribution or dissemination to the country, in the hybridizing of new varieties suitable to various localities, that is the work the Department of Agriculture ought to do; and it ought to get away from the distributing of ordinary varieties of seeds that everybody can get at the corner store, and that was never contemplated by the framers of the law. That is practically the position that I take.

And although it may not be germane to the subject, I am just going to say one word, following my friend Mr. Fottler, on one subject that he referred to.

Grass seeds are mixed in the field as well as in the bins; more in the field than in the bins, as I understand. I am not a seedsman—I am a florist, although I am with a seed house. Seeds come from the farmer just as they are cut from the field. Then seedsmen, as I understand it—you know more about it than I do—have to put it through machinery to cleanse it. Now, the Department of Agriculture may, perhaps, look after the farmer. While it is difficult to decide what seed is mixed in the seed itself without expert examination, any man employed by the Department of Agriculture can go into the field and see the growing stub and can tell at a glance if it is mixed, and if he sees that the field is mixed beyond the legal percentage, let him say to the farmer, " You can not market that."

Senator DOLLIVER. That is a pretty elaborate kind of inspection.

Mr. O'MARA. Now, gentlemen, if there is any question which anyone desires to ask me—otherwise, I think I have said all I care to.

Senator DOLLIVER. These seedsmen are complaining because their business is interfered with; but, as I understand it, the Department is simply one of their customers. They deal with the Department at their wholesale rates, do they not—the seedsmen scattered throughout the country?

Mr. O'MARA. I will put it in this way: Peter Henderson & Co., for instance, were at one time doing a wholesale trade, and also a retail trade. We found the more we sold to the jobber the more we were losing. We cut the jobber out, and the seedsmen of the country, perhaps, would like to cut the Government out, the Government being a wholesale buyer, and sell to the retailer.

Senator DOLLIVER. After these seeds leave the producer, supposing them to be first-class seeds, is it not a fact that they deteriorate rapidly? And I think I am correct in saying that on every corner in the town I live in there has been the same box of seeds sitting out for the last twenty seasons. There is no guaranty that the seeds are new, is there?

Mr. O'MARA. That is a field with which I am not familiar. I will answer you as best I can.

Senator MONEY. Is it not a fact that the seedsmen send around and get these old seeds and have them returned to them, as a general thing?

Mr. O'MARA. I understand in a general way that the leading distributors of boxes have a representative in each county, who goes around and collects the boxes at the end of the season.

Mr. DOLLIVER. And they send them back the next season?

Senator PERKINS. I also infer from your very interesting discussion of the question that you emphasize the further idea that the people are not getting value received from the Government for what it is costing the Government in the way of the distribution of seeds?

Mr. O'MARA. I believe they are not, because of the wastage.

I have devoted some time to a perusal of the Congressional Record—I have it only from April 24 to May 2 of this year, inclusive—my object being to set at rest the question I raised, whether or not the Department of Agriculture was empowered by law to purchase in the United States new and valuable varieties of seeds, plants, bulbs, etc., and distribute same by any method. My investigations resulted in finding a statement made by Mr. Davis, of Minnesota (vol. 40, No. 112, p. 6273), as follows: " There is no law authorizing the purchase of new and uncommon seeds upon the statute books at the present time." This bears out the statement I made, that to my personal knowledge from written statements which came before me in the course of business, at least two originators of new fruits had offered same for sale to the Department of Agriculture, and were informed by the Department that they were not authorized by law to make such purchases.

Mr. Wadsworth's amendment to the agricultural appropriation bill authorizes only " the purchase and collection from foreign countri

and our possessions of rare and uncommon seeds, plants, bulbs, etc."
Mr. Lamb's amendment, which I understand was finally embraced in
the foregoing, made the same geographical limitations, so that the
domestic hybridizer or discoverer of new and uncommon seeds, plants,
bulbs, etc., is shut out from any prospective benefit under the proposed
law.

My investigation developed another fact to which I beg leave to
call your attention. It is this—Mr. Lamb's amendment begins: " Purchase and distribution of valuable seeds." In several places throughout the amendment covering the free distribution of seeds, plants,
etc., the regular, unadulterated, free Congressional distribution of
garden seeds the word " valuable " is used. The closing paragraph
of said amendment covers the original purport of the enabling act, to
wit: The purchase and distribution of new and valuable seeds, etc.,
but only from foreign countries. It would seem, therefore, that even
in the mind of Mr. Lamb the word " valuable " is subject to a dis-
tinction. It seems to me that the use of the word applied to the purchase and distribution of the ordinary seeds sent out in the free distribution is either an attempt to give them a value they do not possess,
or is a tricky attempt to synchronize the distribution with the original law. If either is the case, it is unworthy of the Government. To
make my meaning clearer, let me say that the Early Rose potato
when it was first introduced and sold at $5 per pound would be a
" valuable " variety in construing the language of the act, but would
not be so construed to-day when it is sold for much less than that per
barrel at every country store. As Burns said:

> Ask why God made the gem so small,
> And why so huge the granite?
> Because God meant mankind should set
> The higher value on it.

It seems to me that the use of the word " valuable," therefore, as
applied to the ordinary garden seeds distributed, leaves the act open
to severe criticism. In the seedmen's catalogues it is the custom to
group novelties and designate them as " New, rare, and valuable
sorts." Established varieties, which have been widely distributed
are relegated to the " General list of standard sorts."

The free distribution of common garden seeds is not sound public
policy, in my opinion; it begets a spirit of mendicancy foreign to
American institutions; if Congress persists in carrying it on, at least
let it be free from the taint of bunco.

Mr. LANDRETH. Gentlemen, I will next introduce Mr. W. Atlee
Burpee, of Philadelphia.

STATEMENT OF W. ATLEE BURPEE.

Mr. BURPEE. Mr. Chairman and gentlemen, the question was asked
here whether the Department of Agriculture had authority to distribute new and rare seeds. There seemed to be a little doubt in Mr.
O'Mara's mind whether the reason they did not distribute them was
for the lack of law or the lack of means. The reason that more new
and rare seeds and plants are not distributed is because the Department has not the money. The position of the seedsmen in opposing
the distribution of common garden and flower seeds has been consist-
t for many years. Our firm was very much criticised in the last

year of Cleveland's Administration. We had the contract for the Atlantic States and also the Pacific States, amounting to some $50,000. Those seeds were packeted and sent out from Philadelphia.

The Hon. J. Sterling Morton, Secretary of Agriculture at that time, whom I knew very well, and myself agitated considerably against the promiscuous distribution of common seeds at that time. Mr. Smith, in charge of the Botanical Gardens here, published a letter which was sent to every Senator and Representative. criticising Hon. J. Sterling Morton and myself for taking the Government money and doing what we did not approve of doing. In answer to Mr. Smith, I told him that Hon. J. Sterling Morton needed no defense at my hands; that as for our contract with the Government it called for seeds and seeds only, and we were supplying the seeds, but that our opinions were not purchasable; that it would have been very bad taste on my part to criticise the Government distribution of common seeds when my neighbors, Landreth & Co., had the contract the year previous. We sent out as good seeds as we could, but the common varieties, and our neighbors did the same thing, and when our firm had the contract I though it was very good taste for us to try to educate the people that they ought not to want 5-cent packages of seeds of common vegetables and ordinary flowers.

When the Hon. James Wilson first became Secretary of Agriculture it was not known to seedsmen for many years whether he believed that this continued distribution of common seeds was advisable or not. I have had the pleasure of having Mr. Wilson at my trial grounds in Doylestown, Bucks County, Pa., but it has only been within the last three or four months that I personally have known how decided his opposition now is against the distribution of common seed. I had the pleasure of calling upon Mr. Wilson early in March, this year, and as I was leaving him he asked several others and myself to step to the greenhouses and see some of the trials of lettuces, including some cross fertilization that was being done with lettuce under glass. We had been discussing the quality of seeds sent out by the Government and also by private firms. Almost every week, of course, we receive letters of complaint against other seedsmen. We receive them against nearly every seedsman. No one firm can satisfy all customers, the soil and conditions has so much to do, but the next week after my return home I received a peculiarly bitter letter against the United States Department of Agriculture. The writer of the letter who sent an order for seed to us said that last year he made a great mistake—that he had so many of the Agricultural Department seeds that he planted a whole garden with them, but that he would never do so again. I thought that was a good opportunity to send to Mr. Wilson this letter, as being in the line of our conversation, and I wrote him as follows:

MARCH 14, 1906.

Hon. JAMES WILSON,
    Secretary of Agriculture, Washington, D. C.

DEAR SIR: Referring to our conversation when I had the pleasure of calling upon you last week, I think you may be interested in the remarks on the inclosed order for seeds.

This will show you that notwithstanding the extreme care that your Department and the leading seedsmen are taking with seed it is impossible for any one house to satisfy every recipient.

I enjoyed very much seeing the lettuces, of which Mr. Oliver is conducting for you such magnificent trials and experiments. While we have very complete trials at Fordhook in the open ground, I have never seen so many varieties of lettuces grown so magnificently under glass. With the great credit that this work and many other lines has given to your Department, I trust sincerely that the present Congress may give you a larger appropriation for useful work and relieve you of the burden of distributing common garden seeds.

With kindest regards, sincerely, yours,   .

——— ———.

In reply, I received the following letter:

DEPARTMENT OF AGRICULTURE,
OFFICE OF THE SECRETARY,
Washington, D. C., March 15, 1906.

Mr. W. ATLEE BURPEE, *Philadelphia, Pa.*

DEAR SIR: I have your letter of the 14th, inclosing an order from a correspondent of yours, who desires better seeds than we have been able to furnish. I return this inclosure herewith. I hope you will have better luck with him than we did, and that he will be better satisfied with your seeds. I would like to have the impression get abroad in the land that all reputable seedsmen sell more reliable seed than the Government furnishes. This I know can be brought about. I would like to have you gentlemen have all the business of sending out common seeds. We shall find plenty to do along the line of hybridizing and selection to get new plants, and in these directions I think we are doing preliminary work for the seedsmen.

Very truly, yours,

JAMES WILSON, *Secretary.*

Senator MONEY. Does not that show that the seedsmen are sending their worst seeds to the Government and reserving the best for their commercial customers? The Government does not raise seed, does it?

Mr. BURPEE. The Government gets its seeds identically as the seedsmen do.

Senator MONEY. But they have to buy most of their seeds from private seedsmen.

Mr. BURPEE. Every seedsman has to buy, if you use the term " buy " in a special sense. Every seedsman contracts for the production every season of 90 per cent of the seeds that he distributes.

Senator MONEY. I understand.

Mr. BURPEE. For instance, take cauliflower seeds; the business of a seedsman is to examine where the best seed of a particular kind of a vegetable can be obtained. Now, there are certain things we can get in California better than anywhere else.

Senator PERKINS. There are a great many seed growers in Santa Clara County.

Mr. BURPEE. Yes; I know that. The onions in California are fine; the lettuce produced there is the finest in the world, I think; but while the brassica tribe grow magnificently there, the seed is practically useless. Cauliflower seed produced in California will not head five plants out of a hundred. Cauliflower seed produced in the south of France or in southern Italy for 50 or 60 cents a pound grows with great success in England, but we in America to produce the best cauliflower must have the seed grown in some cold northern country like Denmark; in the same way radish and carrot seeds are best grown in France, some beets in France, sugar corn in Connecticut and Ohio. He goes to California for the best lettuce seed. He goes to California commercially also for onions, but unfortunately • the heavy adobe land there often makes the bulbs misshapen, and in order to produce first-class seed the California grower must obtain fresh stock seed every few years. We will send out there 25 pounds of one variety grown in Connecticut or Massachusetts. Bulbs should be produced from that this year. The representative of our firm will examine those bulbs at the proper time and throw out those that are not up to our standard. The others which are up to the standard will be planted to produce seeds. But after those bulbs have produced several generations of seed in California they lose a little of their character unless they are grown in lighter soil; but around Watsonville the land is often heavy adobe, and it flattens the globe onion on the bottom.

Senator MONEY. I want to get back 'to the old point. You buy these seeds from various growers, and you buy them to sell?

Mr. BURPEE. That word " buy " needs explaining, as I have said. We do not buy them, but we have them produced.

Senator MONEY. You get the seeds, and then you sell to the Government?

Mr. BURPEE. In part.

Senator MONEY. In part. You and other seedsmen. I do not mean to attack the seedsmen at all, but you seedsmen get the seed from the best sources you can, and you use an intelligent effort. I appreciate all that. Now, when you get the seed, as I understand it, you sell the worst you have to the Department and the best you have to your commercial customers. It has been stated over and over again that the Department sends out worthless seeds.

Mr. BURPEE. No; I beg your pardon. That was probably true twenty years ago, but it was not true under the Administration of Grover Cleveland or President McKinley, and his Secretary of Agriculture is now Secretary. J. Sterling Morton and James Wilson have both maintained a very high standard of the seeds—not merely the vitality tests, but also the purity tests. Let me explain, for instance, about cauliflower. This system of testing was started under our Democratic friend, J. Sterling Morton, and of course it was new to the Department. They had never had a percentage of growth. In the last year of Cleveland's Administration they put the percentage of growth at 85 per cent for cauliflower. They specified a variety of cauliflower that we had, which was Burpee's Best Early. As soon as I saw that percentage of growth, I wrote to A. J. Pieters, in charge of said investigation, and I said:

It is impossible to get Burpee's Best Early or any cauliflower grown in Denmark with a percentage of growth of 85. The seed is shriveled and does not have the strong vitality of seed produced in the south of France or in Italy. If you must have 85 per cent germination of cauliflower, we should have to give you seed produced in the south of France or in Italy or in California, which will cost perhaps one-third or one-fourth as much, but will not be of any value to anyone.

That was when they first started the percentage. Since then they have got the percentage of germination of the different seeds on a very right basis. Now we supply the Government with small orders—small quantities every year of different things. Those are all sold subject not only to germination tests, but also to purity trials in the field, and to-day the Government supplies as good seed as any seedsman, excepting, perhaps, in this one particular: The seedsmen invariably have their seeds produced for them on contract in the section of country best suited to their development. They send out their inspectors to see that the seeds are true to type and otherwise proper. The Government also does that. In Senator Perkins's State and other sections it deals direct with the farmer. But when a big increase comes (suppose $100,000 should be added to this bill) the Government will then have to go into the open market to buy seeds.

Senator MONEY. They buy of the seedsmen, do they not?

Mr. BURPEE. Yes.

Senator MONEY. Then will the seedsmen give them their good seeds?

Mr. BURPEE. The Government will not take anything else now.

Senator MONEY. That is the point I want to make. It has been stated that the Government sent out bad seeds.

Mr. BURPEE. Oh, no; I think that was a misapprehension. What gentleman said that?

Mr. MAULE. We simply referred to the common varieties. We said the seeds were common seeds.

Mr. MONEY. You did not mean that they were bad seeds?

Mr. MAULE. No; just ordinary, common varieties.

Mr. BURPEE. When we said nothing good had been sent out by the Government, we meant that no new varieties had been sent out.

Mr. BURPEE. I am introducing a crimson escholtzia. It is a very beautiful flower. If the Government would send out a new flower like that, or some new vegetable—Mr. Kinney has originated a very fine bean, for which we paid him some hundreds of dollars—if the Government sent out new things of that sort, and taught the people how they could beautify their homes and improve the quality of the vegetables in their gardens, it would be a very beneficial thing. If the Government could pay such men as Mr. Burbank for the investigations which they conduct, I am confident that the results which would be obtained would justify the expenditure.

Senator MONEY. It is not your contention, then, that the Department has been sending out bad seed?

Mr. BURPEE. Oh, no; not at all. They have simply sent out common varieties. In reading the Congressional Record there were some twelve seedsmen who felt very badly, indeed, about a colored lady in the South who wrote the Hon. John Wesley Gaines that she was not able to work to earn money to buy seeds, and she did want a package of blood turnip beet seed and a package of four-o'clocks. Mr. Gaines published this in the Congressional Record, and also a letter from the Secretary of Agriculture that the seed had all been distributed, and we were all so sorry that we said we would each send her a package of four-o'clocks and a package of blood turnip beet seed. Mr. Bolgiano, of Washington, went right down to his office and sent not only that, but some cantaloupe and muskmelon seed and several varieties of seeds, so that poor old lady will get them.

Mr. LANDRETH. I wish now to introduce Mr. Henry W. Wood.

STATEMENT OF MR. HENRY W. WOOD.

Mr. WOOD. It has been mentioned on several occasions in the debate on this subject that this distribution of seeds is something that keeps the Department of Agriculture in touch with the farmers. It seems to me that the Government does more for the farmers than for any other class. Take the whole appropriation that is made for the Department of Agriculture, it is for the benefit of the farmers. The Department issues bulletins on all subjects. It sends out experts to examine diseases of fruit trees; it sends out experts to examine the diseases of cattle; it sends out experts to report on various things, all for the benefit of the farmers. I do not know any class of people in this country who receive the benefits from the Government that the farmers do.

The Senator from Mississippi said something about receiving a large number of requests for seeds. Now, I think it is a matter of common experience that anything that is given away, as soon as people know it they always want it. We issued a little celluloid bookmark as an advertisement, costing 2 cents. We received a request from a little girl in New Orleans for one of these bookmarks, and we sent it to her. After that we received, by actual count, 163 requests for bookmarks to be sent to New Orleans. It is just in that way that you receive a very large number of requests for seeds, and the only wonder to me is that you are not simply overwhelmed with them, because anything that is free you know how it spreads. Even the school girls and children and everybody that can write will be sending for it. It does look to me as though here was a chance to get rid of the whole thing, so far as the distribution of these common seeds is concerned. It certainly does seem to me that the committee ought to be glad to stop that whole thing and turn the expenditure to the experimental stations, with the idea of distributing new, rare, and valuable seeds, and they are the channels which will do good.

Mr. LANDRETH. I will next introduce Mr. William Henry Maule, of Philadelphia.

STATEMENT OF WILLIAM HENRY MAULE, ESQ.

Mr. MAULE. Mr. Chairman, there is one ground which the delegation has not covered that I think ought to be brought to the attention of the committee. These packages of seed on the table there, the Government put them up for less than a cent and a quarter apiece. Now, how does the Government do that? I have been in business nearly thirty years. In order to get our best onion seed we have to make in California, in the Santa Clara Valley, five-year contracts. I have now several contracts that have three or four years to run. In making these contracts for onion seed we have to do so on the basis of 45 to 50 cents a pound. At times these people have raised more onion seed than we need, and the same thing that applies to onion seed also applies to every other variety of seed. The grower has a surplus.

This state of affairs happened two years ago. We could not take all this seed that they raised, and the result was that after disposing of all of it abroad and at home that could be disposed of, several thousand pounds, ten or twenty thousand pounds, of this onion seed was shipped to Washington and sold to the Department of Agriculture at 17 cents a pound, and it was the same seed identically that I and other men had paid 45 and 50 cents a pound for. Now, the Department is not limited. It can get onion seed one year, it can get beet seed another year, and can divide these common seeds up, so it is a very serious menace to the trade, admitting all the while that the seeds are first class. One of our largest growers in the country, Mr. Kinney, will have a thousand bushels of beans, a surplus of good beans. He will come to Washington and say, " Mr. Secretary," or " Mr. Pieters, I have these beans. They are excellent beans; I have a surplus and you can have them at a low figure."

Do not understand me as suggesting that this makes the Government a dumping ground for poor seed. That is not the fact. They are good seeds, but they are surplus seeds, and that is one reason why the Government can put its seeds out at a trifling expense. It is a terrible menace to our trade. One package of seed is a very small thing, but the total is tremendous. The Government sends these seeds through the mails without the payment of postage. There are no expenses of light, heat, power, rent, and so forth, to be added to the cost. In addition to that, here is absolutely the same seed for which I contract to pay the grower my good money—45 to 50 cents a pound— and the Government gets it for 17 cents. That happened in the case of these onion seeds, a great many thousand pounds of them, as I have told you. It was because there was a surplus.

Then I can relate another instance. Some years ago I introduced a new variety of onion called the Prize Taker, and I paid almost a thousand dollars for a very few pounds—not over 50 pounds—of the seed. We sold them for 25 cents a package, five packages for a dollar. A short time after that the Government distributed a very large number of packages of what they called the Prize Taker onion. When those seeds which had been distributed by the Government matured it was found that the onion seed that had been distributed by the Department was nothing but the common Yellow Globe Danvers onion. I wrote to the Department about it, and had the satisfaction of receiving a reply from the Department of Agriculture saying they were very sorry, but that the man had sold them the seed for Prize Taker onion. Now, there were three or four hundred thousand packages of this onion seed into which I had put a thousand dollars. The man who gets a package of this seed from the Government naturally said this Prize Taker onion is no good. Can you not see the injustice that was done?

Now, the most of the seeds that are sent out by the Government are very good seeds, but they are procured at a low price to a very considerable extent, in the way I have stated. If a man has a surplus, he wants to dispose of it. If Mr. Kenney has three or four thousand bushels of beans, I can not blame him for offering them to the Department at a low price. In that way the Department gets a very good seed at a cheap rate. And because there is no limit on the seeds that the Department shall distribute one year it can send out beans, and another year onions, and another year sugar corn, or whatever it can get at the best price.

Senator MONEY. The man who sold bogus onion seeds to the Department is a bad seedsman, is he not?

Mr. MAULE. That was some grower. The Department said they were very sorry, but it did not do me very much good. I have the letter on file. They said it was entirely a misapprehension. They thought it was Prize Taker onion seed. At the time it was distributed I was getting about 15 cents a package for mine. But my main object in addressing you, Mr. Chairman and gentlemen, was to bring to your attention the menace to our trade which results from the

Government being able to buy these surplus seeds at 15 or 17 cents a pound, being the same seed for which we pay as much as 50 cents a pound under our contract. Of course the seed that the Government got in this way was good seed, but it gives you an idea how the Government is able to send out so many packages of seed for such a comparatively small amount of money.

Mr. LANDRETH. Mr. Chairman, the concluding argument on this subject will be made by Mr. William Wolff Smith, of Washington, D. C., who has some letters and papers which he would also like to submit to the committee.

Senator MONEY. Mr. Chairman, I would like to have it understood that these gentlemen who have addressed us this morning have the privilege of extending their remarks if they wish to do so.

The CHAIRMAN. Certainly.

STATEMENT OF WILLIAM WOLFF SMITH, ESQ., OF WASHINGTON. D. C.

Mr. Chairman and gentlemen of the committee, the seed trade of the United States, including the growers of seed and the wholesale and retail dealers therein, through their authorized representatives, present here to-day, desire to respectfully enter as strong a protest as they are capable of making against that portion of the pending agricultural appropriation bill beginning at line 24 on page 20 and extending to line 23 on page 23, inclusive. They do this not altogether from selfish motives, but on the broad ground that the free distribution of seeds is contrary to public policy and an interference with a legitimate industry, unwarranted either by law or justice—an interference, we might add, conspicuous as the only one of its kind in this country, and, as far as we can learn, in the whole world. In other words, the United States is the only country which distributes anything to its citizens free, year after year, and the only articles which are thus distributed are seeds. Therefore, is it not most natural and highly proper for those who make the growing and selling of seeds their sole business to protest against the Government of the great United States, with unlimited money, competing with them in their business and not only giving the seeds away through one Department, but utilizing another to place them in the very hands of the recipients of its benefactions?

It is true that the amount appropriated for the Congressional distribution in this section is only $242,000, the same as last year, of which only a portion will be expended in the purchase of seeds, presumably the same as last year, when $90,000 worth of seeds were purchased. The remainder of the appropriation will be consumed in packeting them and in salaries, traveling expenses, and incidental expenses connected with this distribution. Ninety thousand dollars' worth of seeds is but a small portion of the whole amount of seeds handled yearly, and the seed trade could stand it comfortably if it were not for the uncertainty directly arising from the distribution, which is absolutely demoralizing to the entire seed trade of the country.

It is a well-known practice for some members of Congress to exchange their quotas of seeds for public documents. That is, a city member, whose constitutents have no place to plant the seeds and no fowls to which they can feed them, will bargain with another from a rural district, exchanging his seeds for certain documents for which No. 2's constituents have no use. In this manner I have known members of the House to secure 50,000 and 60,000 packages of seeds from a single distribution. They dump these into their districts and demoralize the whole seed trade therein. We might go into this feature in more detail, but I think it is unnecessary, for you can easily see how extremely annoying this practice is to the entire seed trade, for what affects the retailer affects the wholesaler, and, in turn, the grower.

So much for the seed trade, and we beg to say, Mr. Chairman, that this trade is very extensive, although so scattered that concerted action is impossible. Seeds are sold at almost every country store, by a hundred thousand druggists, and even by the department stores all over the country. Consequently what affects the seed trade affects all of these interests more or less.

That they have a right to oppose legislation so hostile to their interests no fair-minded man will deny. Much was said in the debate in the lower House criticising the seedmen for opposing this appropriation. I do not think there has been a single interest of importance which has not been represented before the Congressional committees at some time or other, either favoring or opposing legislation of some character. That applies to the railroads, the shipbuilders, labor organizations, tobacco, sugar, butter, salt, cement, hides and leather, and a thousand others. But when the seed merchants come along and lift a feeble voice against the interference of the Government in their business—the only one case of its kind in this country, and this country the only one in the world where such is the case— they are denounced as "kid-gloved, spike-tailed agriculturists," who "farm the farmer," and one impetuous member even went so far as to term them "thieves."

Why, Mr. Chairman, if the United States Government were to undertake to distribute a thousand pianos a year, or a hundred thousand pairs of suspenders, or half a million pairs of shoes, the pandemonium which raged in the House over the free-seed distribution would be relegated to the side-show class.

NO SEED TRUST.

Mr. Chairman, when all arguments failed, a "trust" was discovered. A trust in a product that can be raised in any back yard in the country! Yet not an active "trust," but a possible "trust;" one which can be prevented only by distributing a certain portion of its product free. Thus we have a new solution for the ever-present trust problem. Give away a hundred thousand tons of steel rails each year and break the steel trust; a million pounds of sugar and annihilate the sugar trust; a few tons of cigarettes and the American Tobacco Company is out of business; a suitable number of gallons of kerosene and nail the hide of the octopus gigantea to the walls of the Capitol! The gentlemen present in behalf of the seed trade will enter their denial of any combination, present or prospective, although the idea is too ridiculous to be entertained.

ENTIRE COUNTRY OPPOSED TO FREE SEEDS.

But, Mr. Chairman, the seed trade, although the only business interest concerned, is not alone in its opposition to this appropriation. We venture to say that no practice is more universally and, we believe, justly condemned by the country at large than the one complained of. The press is practically a unit in opposition to it. We base this assertion on the fact that of thousands of clippings we have never received even one which favored the distribution.

The charge has been made against the seedsmen—this bogie " trust "—that they control the press through their advertising. Does any intelligent man believe that papers like the New York Sun, Herald, Times, Tribune, World, and Journal, the daily newspapers of Philadelphia, Boston, Chicago, St. Louis, Washington, and other cities, without regard to political affiliations and without exception, could each and every one be controlled through their advertising columns? Yet no one can produce from any of these newspapers an editorial approving the miscellaneous distribution of garden seeds.

The foregoing applies equally to the agricultural press. If there was any class of publications in which the seedsmen would naturally advertise it would be in the agricultural press.

If these publications did not reflect their subscribers' sentiments they would have no subscribers. Therefore when they condemn this practice it is reasonable to presume their readers are in sympathy with them.

Mr. Chairman, we have here a thousand editorials and clippings relating to the free-seed distribution. They have been hurriedly collected, for until the House Committee on Agriculture voted to omit this item from the bill none of the seedsmen entertained the hope that Congress would abandon the practice at this time.

I also have here letters from agricultural papers, received in the last few days, since it was stated in the House of Representatives that the farmers were in favor of this free-seed distribution. The clippings to which I have referred are from agricultural and daily papers in all parts of the country.

Senator PERKINS. In every State?

Mr. SMITH. Every State.

Senator PERKINS. From the Southern States?

Mr. SMITH. All through the South. The South is unusually hostile to it. And I may say to the Senator from Mississippi that since the southern members in Congress led the opposition to the abolition of this seed distribution the southern papers have come out and said it was a crying shame that the South should be responsible for the continuance of such a petty little graft as this.

Senator MONEY. I should be very glad if you would quote any paper from Mississippi that said that.

Mr. SMITH. I have none from Mississippi.

Senator MONEY. I have many that talk the other way.

Mr. MAULE. The Agricultural Journal, of Stockville, Miss., printed an editorial opposing it very strongly.

Senator MONEY. I have not seen that.

Senator PERKINS. Mr. Simmons, a member of this committee, and a Senator from North Carolina, says, as I understand, that the people are generally in favor of seed distribution, and I think Mr.

Latimer, of South Carolina, who is also a member of the committee, has said the same thing.

Mr. SMITH. I have personally inspected a great many clippings on this subject, and I have never seen a clipping of any kind from any paper that has ever favored this distribution. I will submit a list of papers, arranged by States, and also submit a great many letters from agricultural papers in the South, saying that they have been fighting this thing for years. I remember one editor said his paper was founded twenty-three years ago, and that he had been fighting this ever since it was founded, and that he was going to keep on fighting it until it was defeated or he died. One thing to which I wish to call especial attention. Representative Gaines, of Tennessee, presented to the House two letters, ostensibly from editors. He had them inserted in the Record, as coming, I think, from the editor of the Nashville Banner and the Nashville American. I took it for granted that they were from the editors of those papers, but in looking through the clippings I found editorials from the Nashville Banner and the Nashville American, both bitterly denouncing this distribution. I said to myself, " That is rather peculiar, coming from the editor of a paper that wrote to Mr. Gaines indorsing this thing and asking for seeds." So I wrote to the Nashville Banner. I did not know the editor's name, but simply wrote to the editor of the Nashville Banner, and I said, " Here is a letter purporting to be signed by you, printed in the Congressional Record." I got this telegram in reply yesterday:

Sears is not editor. The Banner opposes free-seed distribution.

G. H. BASKETT, *Editor.*

Since then I have learned from the correspondent of the Banner here that Mr. Sears is the office boy in the Banner office, and that he wrote on the office paper. [Laughter.]

The following editorials from the Nashville American and the Nashville Banner will, I think, effectually refute those two letters from alleged editors, the only ones that were produced:

[American, Nashville, Tenn., March 23, 1906.]

CONGRESSMEN AND SEEDS.

There is a general feeling that the Department of Agriculture, in carrying out Congressional instructions, is wasting a good deal of time and money in the distribution of seed. These seed, in the manner and form now sent out by Congressmen, do not fall in good ground. In the vast majority of cases, not in the ground at all. Nowadays educated farmers who receive these rattling packages coming, maybe for aught of any germinating power they show, from Joseph's Egyptian granary, smile at the thought that their diligent Representative is not only trying in a gentle way to work them, but is actually overworking the mails. If reliable statistics could be had, it would doubtless appear that the results obtained wholly fail to meet the actual cost to the Government of transmission. Good farmers pay the closest attention to the selection of good seed, for this is the very basis of success. They much prefer to buy their seed from reliable dealers whose representations and guaranties carry weight.

[The Banner, Nashville, Tenn., April 23, 1906.]

FREE SEEDS.

The House Committee on Agriculture, in reporting the agricultural appropriation bill, has omitted the usual item covering the Congressional free distribution of vegetable and flower seeds. The committee in its report says there is not and never has been any warrant of law for such expenditure, and the item has heretofore simply been tolerated. The purpose of the law authorizing the distribution of "rare and uncommon seeds" was, says the committee, solely for experiment through the experiment stations in the several States, and this feature has been retained in the appropriation bill reported.

The cutting out of the free-seed distribution appropriation is a move of genuine reform. It will prevent a useless and extravagant waste. The Congressional distribution of seeds has become a costly farce and a mere means of electioneering.

Senator MONEY. Do you include the Augusta Chronicle in your list of papers?

Mr. SMITH. Yes; the Augusta Chronicle Publishing Company. In answer to a letter sent to them, calling attention to the action of the committee and asking them to support it, they say:

We will take pleasure in giving editorial attention to this matter and in doing what we can with our own Representatives in Congress.

Senator MONEY. The reason I ask that is because that editor, Mr. Walsh, is a particular friend of mine, who used to be in this Senate, and voted for garden seeds every time.

Mr. SMITH. I think these letters and editorials show how the press looks at the matter, and other letters which I will later submit will show how the public regards it. But, if there should be any lingering doubt upon the subject, permit me to call your attention to the attitude of the National Grange, the subordinate granges, and agricultural societies of all kinds. Can the most enthusiastic friend of the farmer produce a resolution from such an organization favoring these prize penny packages? No, sir; not one. You have previously heard from ex-Governor Bachelder as to what the National Grange has said on this subject, and in a recent letter Mr. Bachelder also said:

Replying to your favor of March 27 in regard to the elimination of the free-seed distribution by the Government, will say that this movement has the support of the National Grange. The legislative committee of the National Grange will meet in Washington and will aid in sustaining the report of the committee if in any way possible.

I also submit the following resolutions and protests from granges and agricultural societies:

Hon. R. R. HITT,
   Representative from Illinois to House of Representatives:

As there was some discussion during the last Congress as to the appropriation for the free distribution of seeds to farmers, we, the undersigned farmers and voters, pray that you will give the following your consideration:

As that appropriation was created to distribute rare and uncommon seeds and as it only distributes common seeds that can be purchased by the farmer for two (2) or three (3) cents a packet, it is therefore only an expense to the United States Government and of no practical benefit to the farmer.

And as the Government is annually running millions in debt in order that the farmer may have a rural mail delivery, which is of some benefit, we, the undersigned farmers, pray that you use your influence to abolish the above-named appropriation.

Richard N. Kelley, Ernest J. Siegel, Oliver H. Long, Poley Clay, Geo. R. Randall, Wm. Holland, Joe M. Farrell, J. B. Fox, Geo. Lepper, L. E. Russell.

The following was adopted at the thirty-fourth annual session of the State Grange of Illinois, December 12-14, 1905, and we request your favorable attention thereto:

Resolved, As practical and independent farmers, that we call upon Congress to abolish its petty, annoying, and needless practice of broadcasting free and common garden seeds all over the rural districts, and that the control of seed distribution be placed under the Department of Agriculture and limited to experimental work.

OLIVER WILSON, *Master*,
JEANNETTE E. YATES, *Secretary*,
Illinois State Grange.

Resolution adopted at the annual meeting of the Minnesota State Agricultural Society, in Minneapolis, in January, relating to free seed is as follows:

Resolved, That, in our judgment, Congress should cease appropriating public money to pay for the distribution of seeds, and our Representatives in Congress are requested to use their influence to this sensible end.

E. W. RANDALL, *Secretary.*

John S. Crawford, Patrick Crosby, M. E. Stemler, Alfred Woolley, E. Lyle, L. H. Stemler, S. Crine, G. Heiser, Chas. H. Ludwig, J. H. Douglass, C. C. Hulsat, L. Giese, L. Ott, James Meinzer, Jacob Matthews, Hollie Matthews, John Ott.

We, the above-signed officers, etc., of Olive Branch Grange, desire to be placed on record as being against the free distribution of seeds, and respectfully ask you to use your influence against the same.

JOHN S. CRAWFORD,
Secretary, Matawan, N. J.

Resolution adopted by the twentieth annual closing Wisconsin Farmers' Institute, held at Plymouth March 13, 14, and 15, 1906.

Resolved, That the Round-up Farmers' Institute of Wisconsin urge the Congressmen and Senators from Wisconsin to vote to abolish the free distribution of common seeds by the Government and to favor the appropriation of more money in the introduction of valuable new seeds and plants and in the improvement of plants and animals by breeding.

HORTICULTURAL SOCIETY OF NEW YORK,
New York City, March 26, 1906.

Hon. TIMOTHY D. SULLIVAN,
    Washington, D. C.

MY DEAR SIR: At the regular meeting of the Horticultural Society of New York, held on March 14, the subjoined resolution was presented in council and unanimously adopted. Acting under instructions from the council, I beg leave to transmit copy of said resolution to you:

Resolved, That we view with satisfaction the probable discontinuance of the free distribution of garden seeds by the United States Government. We respectfully urge upon our Representatives in Congress and the United States Senators from New York that they use their best efforts to have this practice stopped. We denounce it as a useless waste of public money and flagrant perversion of the aims and intent of the law creating the Department of Agriculture.

Yours, faithfully,

LEONARD BARRON, *Secretary.*

NEW YORK, *March 15, 1906.*

Hon. GEO. H. LINDSAY,
    House of Representatives, Washington, D. C.

DEAR SIR: At a regular meeting of the New York Florists' Club, at which 150 members were present, I was instructed, by the unanimous vote of the club, to send you a copy of the following resolutions:

Whereas, having learned through the public press that the Committee on Agriculture in Congress have stricken out the appropriation for the distribution of free seeds, we desire to express our approval of said action.

Resolved, That we urge upon our Representatives in Congress that they do all within their power to sustain the action of the committee.

Resolved, That a copy of these resolutions be sent to the Senators from New York and our Representatives in Congress.

Yours, respectfully,

JOHN YOUNG, *Secretary.*

ELLINGTON GRANGE,
Ellington, Conn., April 24, 1906.

Hon. E. S. HENRY, *Washington, D. C.:*

At a meeting of Ellington Grange, No. 46, held March 28, your position on the free-seed question was heartily indorsed by all present.

Very truly, yours,

J. M. MARKS, *Secretary.*

UNIONTOWN, PA., *March, 1906.*

Hon. A. F. COOPER, *M. C.*

SIR: We, the members of the Union Farmers' Club of Fayette County, Pa., a list of whose names is herewith inclosed, hereby request that you use your influence and endeavors against the agricultural free-seed distribution, except in regards to the testing and sending out of new and rare seeds and plants.

The above was placed before the club at its regular meeting March 24, 1906, and adopted by a unanimous vote.

W. B. SWEARINGEN, *President.*
A. C. OGLEVEE, *Secretary.*

COMMITTEE ON THE DISTRICT OF COLUMBIA,
HOUSE OF REPRESENTATIVES, UNITED STATES,
Washington, D. C., March 15, 1906.

Hon. J. W. WADSWORTH,
Chairman Committee on Agriculture, House of Representatives.

MY DEAR SIR: Inclosed find a communication from my district signed by thirty farmers, returning seeds sent to them. I believe their position is entirely correct.

Yours, very truly,

J. W. BABCOCK.

[Inclosure.]

LA VALLE LODGE, AMERICAN SOCIETY OF EQUITY,
La Valle, Wis., —— —, 1906.

Hon. J. W. BABCOCK, *Washington, D. C.*

DEAR SIR: We, farmers of this vicinity, known as the "American Society of Equity," have turned down the free-seed distribution, and we have decided not to accept them, which we return to you.

The seeds are not reliable, and we think it a waste of time and money to use them.

We would rather have the money appropriated for good roads, and we petition you to give this your attention and do all you can to have such a move brought about. Thanking you for past favors, we remain yours for equity.

[Signed by thirty farmers.]

THE NEW YORK STATE POULTRY SOCIETY,
Watervliet, N. Y., April 9, 1906.

Hon. W. W. COCKS,
House of Representatives, Washington, D. C.

HONORABLE SIR: Myself, as well as the majority of the members of the above association, which I represent, are opposed to the distribution of common garden seeds, but do favor the distribution of seeds of new plants for trial. Trusting this will meet with your approval.

Very truly, yours,

JOHN D. JAQUINS, *Presid----*

NEW YORK STATE FRUIT GROWERS' ASSOCIATION,
Penn Yan, N. Y., March 31, 1906.
Hon. W. W. COCKS,
Washington, D. C.

DEAR SIR: I learn that you are interested in a plan to abolish the present seed distribution, so far as it applies to common garden seeds. I wish to say that my acquaintance with the farmers of this section of the State, and with the fruit growers of the whole State, leads me to the belief that the sentiment is strongly in favor of the movement for which you stand.

Personally, for many years I have been opposed to Government seed distribution. It might be desirable to send the seeds of certain new plants into localities where the probable conditions would be favorable for them, but for the present I believe that the whole plan had best be discontinued.

Anything you do along this line, I believe, will be appreciated by the farmers and fruit growers of New York State.

Very truly, yours,   E. C. GILLETT, *Secretary.*

NEW YORK STATE ASSOCIATION OF BEE KEEPERS' SOCIETIES,
Clifton Springs, N. Y., April 3, 1906.
Hon. W. W. COCKS,
House of Representatives, Washington, D. C.

DEAR SIR: I am not interested in the sale of seeds; but as an American citizen I wish to protest against a continuance of the Congressional distribution of common and abundant varieties of garden seeds and to urge a discontinuance of the practice, believing as I do that said seeds are of doubtful utility, to say the least.

I am, however, in favor of the Government distribution of seeds of new varieties of plants, and believe that more attention should be given to the testing and distribution of such seeds.

Believing that I voice the sentiment of a large majority of those whom it is my privilege to represent, I would urge you to use your best efforts toward bringing about the desired change in this matter.

Yours, truly,   W. F. MARKS.

HORTICULTURAL SOCIETY OF NEW YORK,
New York City, March 26, 1906.
Hon. WILLIAM W. COCKS,
Washington, D. C.

MY DEAR SIR: At the regular meeting of the Horticultural Society of New York, held on March 14, the subjoined resolution was presented in council and unanimously adopted. Acting under instructions from the council, I beg leave to transmit copy of said resolution to you:

"*Resolved,* That we view with satisfaction the probable discontinuance of the free distribution of garden seeds by the United States Government. We respectfully urge upon our Representatives in Congress, and the United States Senators from New York, that they use their best efforts to have this practice stopped. We denounce it as a useless waste of public money and a flagrant perversion of the aims and intent of the law creating the Department of Agriculture."

Yours, faithfully,

LEONARD BARRON, *Secretary.*

THE NEW YORK STATE SHEEP BREEDERS' ASSOCIATION,
Batavia, N. Y., April 2, 1906.
Hon. W. W. COCKS,
Washington, D. C.

DEAR SIR: I want to express my approval of the determined stand you are taking in opposition to any further distribution of ordinary garden seeds which are sent out from Washington. I have never been able to see one good reason for such distribution as it has been carried on in past years. The seeds which I have received in quite large quantities are as a rule not as desirable varieties, neither are they as fresh as can ordinarily be purchased from reliable seed houses, and whatever seeds have been sent have been used only as food for poultry. I trust you will keep up this fight until the distribution is discontinued, and I am confident that such course on your behalf will merit the approval of the best farmers of the country. At the same time I am, of course, in favor of a reasonable distribution and experimenting with strictly new varieties of seeds, and in this way increase the number of valuable plants that may be adapted to various localities.

With congratulations for your good work in this direction, I remain,

Very truly, yours,

FRANK D. WARD, *President.*

NEW YORK STATE FRUIT GROWERS' ASSOCIATION,
Halls Corners, N. Y., March 31, 1906.

Hon. W. W. COCKS, *Washington, D. C.*

DEAR SIR: I notice by the papers that you are the originator of a bill before Congress to abolish the free distribution of common garden seeds. Personally, I believe you are right, and from what I can learn in meeting the members of the State Fruit Growers' Association I believe it meets with the hearty approval of a large majority of our members. Still I think the careful distribution of the seeds of new varieties of plants and vegetables will continue to be of benefit to agriculture.

Trusting you may succeed in the passage of your bill, I am.

Truly, yours,

T. B. WILSON.

NEW YORK STATE FRUIT GROWERS' ASSOCIATION.
Penn Yan, N. Y., March 31, 1906.

Hon. W. W. COCKS, *Washington, D. C.*

DEAR SIR: I learn that you are interested in a plan to abolish the present seed distribution, so far as it applies to common garden seeds. I wish to say that my acquaintance with the farmers of this section of the State, and with the fruit growers of the whole State, leads to the belief that the sentiment is strongly in favor of the movement for which you stand. Personally, for many years, I have been opposed to Government seed distribution. It might be desirable to send the seeds of certain new plants into localities where the probable conditions would be favorable for them, but for the present I believe that the whole plan had best be discontinued. Anything you do along this line I believe will be appreciated by the farmers and fruit growers of New York State.

Very truly, yours,

——— ———, *Secretary.*

NEW YORK STATE GRANGE, P. OF H.,
Skaneateles, N. Y., February 15, 1906.

Hon. WILLIAM W. COCKS, M. C., *Washington, D. C.*

DEAR SIR: Your esteemed favor of the 13th received and noted. The State Grange did take action relative to the free-seed distribution. They are unanimously opposed to it and have been for a long time. They look upon it as a very useless and extravagant thing to do. Our legislative committee would be pleased to call on any committee at Washington and express these views at any time.

Yours, respectfully,

W. N. GILES.

NEW YORK STATE GRANGE,
OFFICE OF THE MASTER,
Philadelphia, N. Y., April 3, 1906.

Hon. W. W. COCKS, *Washington, D. C.*

DEAR SIR: I take this opportunity of addressing you in regard to the free-seed distribution. It seems to me that this is the proper time to cut off this needless and wasteful use of the public money. For myself, personally, and for the order of Patrons of Husbandry, numbering 70,000 members in the State of New

York, I wish to enter a protest against any further distribution of common seeds by the Federal Government. So far as the distribution of new or rare varieties of seeds is concerned, I think that there is no objection to that, but the practice of sending common seed should be stopped at once.

Yours, very truly,

GEO. A. FULLER.

I also submit a list of publications which have editorially and otherwise protested against free-seed distribution:

Alabama.—Montgomery Advertiser, The Dixie Home.

California.—The California Fruit Grower, The Rural Californian, Town and Country Journal.

Colorado.—The Field and Farm, Ranch and Range.

Connecticut.—Meriden Republican, The Connecticut Farmer, The Bridgeport Standard.

Georgia.—Augusta Gazette-Chronicle, The Columbus Ledger, The Nut Grower, Southern Ruralist Company, The Farmer and Stockman.

Illinois.—Illinois State Journal, The Farmer's Voice; Farm, Field, and Fireside; Elgin Dairy Report, Farmers' Call, Farmers' Review, The Prairie Farmer, Daily National Live Stock Reporter, Maxwell's Talisman, The Breeders' Gazette, Farm Life, Florists' Review.

Indiana.—The Indianapolis News, Crawfordsville Journal, Terre Haute Morning Star, Indiana Farmer, The Farmers' Guide, The American Farmer, The Agricultural Epitomist.

Iowa.—Farmers' Tribune, Kimball's Dairy Farmer.

Kansas.—Kansas Farmer, Farmers' Advocate, The Topeka Capital, Topeka Mail and Breeze.

Kentucky.—Kentucky Farmer and Breeder.

Massachusetts.—The Boston Globe, Hampshire Gazette, Beverly Times, New Bedford Standard, Newburyport News, American Cultivator.

Michigan.—The Detroit Times, The Detroit Journal, Bay City Tribune, The Strawberry, The Michigan Farmer, The Gleaner, The National Fruit Grower.

Minnesota.—Minneapolis Journal, Winona Republican-Herald, Duluth Evening Herald, St. Paul Pioneer Press, Minneapolis Daily News, Farm Implements, The Farmer, The Northwestern Agriculturist; Farm, Stock, and Home; Agricultural Experiments.

Mississippi.—Southern Farm Gazette (Starkville).

Missouri.—The Tri-State Farm Journal, The Modern Farmer, The Fruit Grower, The National Farmer and Stock Grower, The Woman's Farm Journal.

Nebraska.—The Twentieth Century Farmer, Farm Magazine, Omaha Bohemian-American.

New Jersey.—The New Jersey Farmer.

New York.—Syracuse Post-Standard, Albany Argus, Hornellsville Times, Jamestown Post, Utica Press, New York Produce Review, New York Farmer, The Garden Magazine, Poultry Husbandry, Metropolitan and Rural Home.

Ohio.—Dayton Daily News, Akron Democrat, Hamilton Telegraph, Dayton Journal, Farm and Fireside, Cincinnati Commercial Tribune, Cincinnati Enquirer, Ohio State Journal, Ohio Farmer.

Oklahoma.—Oklahoma Farmer.

Oregon.—North Pacific Rural Spirit.

Pennsylvania.—Pittsburg Chronicle Telegraph, Pittsburg Gazette, Philadelphia Inquirer, Philadelphia Record, House and Garden, The Implement Age, National Stockman and Farmer, The Practical Farmer, Farm Journal.

Rhode Island.—Providence Journal.

South Dakota.—South Dakota Farmer (Sioux Falls).

Tennessee.—Southern Agriculturalist.

Texas.—Fort Worth Record, Dennison Herald, Waco Times-Herald, Houston Chronicle, Farm and Ranch, Texas Stockman and Farmer.

Vermont.—St. Albans Messenger.

Virginia.—Norfolk Virginian Pilot, The Southern Planter (Richmond), Norfolk Dispatch.

Washington.—The Ranch, Farm and Home.

West Virginia.—Wheeling Daily News, Wheeling Intelligencer.

Wisconsin.—Marinette Daily Star, The Wisconsin Agriculturalist.

Is it not reasonable to presume that the granges, horticultural societies, and the agricultural press correctly present the views of the only class which anyone has the audacity to say demands these gifts?

Now, Mr. Chairman, I am not one of those who claim "nobody wants the seeds," for I believe many want them. Some people want anything they can get for nothing. But I must say I don't think any self-respecting person who stops to consider that this is charity would stoop to ask his member for a few cents' worth of seeds. But we have heard much of the farmer who follows the plow suffering for the beans, pease, corn, etc., of which a paternal Government sends him about an ounce whenever his Congressman has them to spare. We say the farmer does not want the seeds, and point to his newspapers and the resolutions of his granges, horticultural, and other societies to support our claims. The advocates of free seeds, however, say he does, and a number of letters were produced in the debate to prove their claims. All but one, I believe, were handed in by Mr. Gaines, a member from Tennessee, of whom you may have heard. Here are some of the " farmers " who are demanding free seeds from Mr. Gaines with tears in their voices.

. L. X. Nance, chief operator, N. C. and L. R. R. Mr. Nance submits the names of six other farmers, who prove to be Mrs. A. J. Nance, Mrs. L. M. Nance, Mrs. W. P. Dans, Mrs. E. M. Davis, and Mrs. M. D. Nance, all of them residents of towns. Apparently Farmer Nance was looking out for the family—and permit me to call your attention to a highly significant line in his letter. " Remember me," says Farmer Nance, " as your supporter and admirer." Doubtless the family secured their seeds.

Another " farmer " is Miss Fanny Battle, secretary of the United Charities, of Nashville; another, Miss Mary Woods, secretary of the Centennial Club, of Nashville; another is W. M. Green, of Nashville, who says his " little granddaughter "—presumably also a " farmer "—wants some seeds. Miss Hulda Lyle, of Hackberry, Tenn., is still another.

But a " peach " comes in from John D. Parks, of Port Royal. " I have lots of friends," says Farmer Parks, " who have fed me through our great tobacco fight, and that is one of the main reasons I am so anxious about getting a big lot of seed of all kinds for them." Mr. Chairman, is it exactly a " square deal " that the Government should be called upon to pay Farmer Parks's board bills in seeds?

But listen. Parks wrote again, and he puts up an awful howl. He had received his quota, but it was not enough. " I did not have half to give near all those who had been feeding me and my faithful little horse "—you see he rings in a feed bill for his horse this time—" through our great tobacco fight so long. And now I am bothered no little, for those who have been so faithful to me "—" to me," mark you—" to be expecting something from me they need and not be able to furnish them." Apparently the idea of buying the seeds himself did not occur to Parks.

" When I noticed 38,000,000 packages of seeds would be subject to the order of Representatives for distribution to begin in December," continues Farmer Parks, " I felt encouraged to feel like I would make lots of my good lady friends feel like I was trying to help them, and especially show in efforts and actions I had appreciated what they had done for me." And yet some have the audacity to say this is not a "graft."

Farmer H. C. Singleton, of Nashville; a Mrs. Morris, a Miss Brown, a Mrs. J. W. Hagerwood, Professor Daniel, of Vanderbilt University; Mrs. Castleman, a Mr. Beaumont, whose wife "wishes to have a good garden," and many other ladies and gentlemen complete the list of "farmers."

But, Mr. Chairman, there was one letter produced which made a marked impression on me, opposed as I am to this distribution. It was from Mrs. W. F. Jones, of Antioch, Tenn., who said:

ANTIOCH, TENN., March 1, 1906.

Mr. GAINES.

DEAR FRIEND: I got your free seed last year and they did mighty well, and I thank you for them, and if you have any beet seed to give away I would be thankful if you would send me a paper of the blood-turnip beet seed. I haven't got any and can't get any; and if you have them, send a paper of four-o'clock seed. I am a poor old woman, and have one arm broken, and can't work to buy any seed. Send me the seed, if you please, and oblige a friend. If you send the seed, direct this way: Mrs. W. F. Jones, Antioch, Tenn., R. F. D. No. 16, and oblige a friend, Mrs. W. F. Jones, and if you have them to give away, please send them as soon as you can.

Did this poor woman get her seeds? No, sir; the quota had been exhausted—the seeds had gone to feed Farmer Parks and his faithful little horse.

NO FARMERS ON RECORD AS FAVORING FREE SEEDS.

Now, Mr. Chairman, these were, as I have said, all the letters produced by 153 members of the House to substantiate their claims that the "farmers" are demanding these seeds. Horse feed bills seem to have been paid for with free seeds.

Mr. Chairman, I have said this distribution was against sound public policy. I will go further and say it promotes grafting and corruption—on a small scale, it is true, but the skilled grafter begins with small things and works upward. For a number of years there were tons of seed knocking about in the catacombs below. Why, Mr. Chairman, a peculiar industry flourishes at your very door—it is the business of buying and selling these seeds, which the "lady farmers" of friend Gaines's district so loudly demanded.

A newspaper correspondent related to me the following incident, and it is not three months old. He was anxious to secure certain Government publications, five in number. A member of Congress was anxious to accommodate him, but he was unable to procure them. Arrangements were therefore made with a "huckster" of seeds and documents, by which the member exchanged 5,000 packages of seeds for the desired public documents. Later I learned that another member of Congress who wanted some additional packages of seeds purchased 4,000 of these packages from the same "huckster" at $15 per thousand—a cent and a half apiece!

One more instance: A clerk to a committee told me he sent enough seeds every year to the brother-in-law of his wife to seed his farm. Then he and his wife went there for their vacation and enjoyed the cabbages, turnips, corn, and beans which grew from these seeds.

Now, Mr. Chairman, I maintain, as a plain proposition of equity, that if these seeds are given to a member to distribute it is his duty to see they go to his constituents, and instead of the 5,000 packages being exchanged for documents to accommodate a friend they should have been distributed to the people of the State represented by the member. That the clerk alluded to had no right to seed his wife's brother-in-law's farm at Government expense will be admitted by all.

FREE-SEED DISTRIBUTION UNCONSTITUTIONAL.

Now, Mr. Chairman, I approach with diffidence a phase of this discussion on which I am hardly qualified to speak: Has Congress the right to give these seeds away? We appeal to you, Mr. Chairman and gentlemen of the committee, is there the slightest vestige of authority in the Constitution for this appropriation? We do not believe there is unless it is under the general-welfare clause. Can Congress take the money which belongs to all and constitutionally appropriate it for the benefit of only a small part of the people? We doubt if the students of the Constitution will find any authority vested in Congress to give anything away. Could Congress constitutionally give every man a dollar or every man·a loaf of bread? Perhaps so; but we assert without fear of contradiction that Congress could not constitutionally appropriate money to give half the population a dollar each and the remainder nothing. Yet that is exactly what is being done with seeds. The required population for a Congressional district is now 192,000, yet each member receives only 12,000 packages of seeds, enough for only one out of every sixteen in his district. Now, we maintain the remainder of the residents of his district have a legitimate right to complain of this expenditure.

CLASS LEGISLATION.

And, Mr. Chairman, the only class which is represented as being in favor of this distribution are the farmers. Nowhere have we heard of the locomotive engineers, of the grimy miners, of the carpenters, the mechanics, the boiler makers, the butchers, the bakers, or those engaged in the manufacture of candlesticks. What of them, Mr. Chairman? What does a paternalistic government do for them? Does it give them a plane, a saw, or an oil can, a meat ax, or a razor? No, sir; not even a kind word. Why, then, Mr. Chairman—and we ask this in all seriousness—even if the farmers did want these prize packages, which they do not, why should they be singled out as the sole recipients of the nation's bounty? In the name of the 72,000,000 Americans engaged in other occupations we protest against this discrimination and this " class legislation."

If it is constitutional to give away seeds it is constitutional to give away boots and shoes; and, Mr. Chairman, there are more people in the city of New York to-day suffering for shoes and clothing than there are farmers in the entire United States who either demand or want the packages of seeds.

But, Mr. Chairman, the Constitution of the United States does not warrant the giving away of anything which depends on favor. If I want seeds and my Congressman does not give them to me, I go without. My neighbor gets them, and the Government gives him something it does not give to me. I do not believe that is constitutional—it assuredly is not justice.

You are all familiar with the fact that a Senator or member can send one frank to the Department of Agriculture and have 50 or 100 of these packages sent in bulk to one address. To see how that works out, let us suppose a case. A and B are truck gardeners, adjacent farms and the same market. A stands in with the Congressman—" a supporter and admirer," as one of the Tennessee " farmers " said. A gets a lot of seed, the finest selected seed his Congressman can procure—at Government expense. B gets nothing and pays for his seed. Is not the Government unduly favoring A at the expense of B and giving him an advantage, no matter how slight, over his competitor in the truck-farming business? Why, Mr. Chairman, there is no doubt of it. Is this legal? Is this constitutional?

Mr. Chairman, we now approach another feature of this business. Is the free-seed distribution of practical assistance to agriculture? Suppose it were. Would it be justifiable? To these questions we can not but answer emphatically " No." The distribution of a thousand specially bred stallions and mares every year might improve the breeding of horses in this country, but who would seriously champion an appropriation for this purpose and who would get the horses? This bill carries a large appropriation to investigate dairying conditions, but no one proposes to promiscuously distribute a lot of Holsteins or Jerseys. But we think a little investigation and a little applied common sense will demonstrate that this distribution is of no practical good to agriculture. We waive the point that several millions of these packages are assigned to members whose constituents can utilize them only in flower pots, and pass to what the Secretary of Agriculture says on this subject. So many inquiries have been made of the Department of Agriculture as to its attitude that Secretary Wilson had an extract from his annual report of 1903 reprinted, and to inquirers he incloses the same. I quote a letter from Professor Galloway, accompanying the extract:

The views of this Department with reference to the distribution of miscellaneous vegetable and flower seeds have been clearly set forth in our various reports. The attitude of the Department was stated by the Secretary in his report for 1903, extract from which I send inclosed.

The extract says:

With regard to securing and distributing miscellaneous garden and flower seeds, the fact remains that this work does not accomplish the ends for which the law was originally framed. There are collected, put up, and distributed now, on Congressional orders, nearly 40,000,000 packets of such seeds each year. These seeds are the best that can be obtained in the market, but from the fact that large numbers of packets are wanted the seed obtained can be of standard sorts only, such as are to be found everywhere for sale in the open market. As there is no practical object to be gained in distributing this kind of seed, it seems desirable that some change be made. To this end it would seem wise to limit our work entirely to securing and distributing seeds, plants, etc., of new and rare sorts * * *. This is a line of work that would result in much more value to individual districts throughout the country than the distribution of a large quantity of common varieties of garden seed, which have no particular merits so far as newness or promise are concerned.

In a letter to Representative James A. Tawney, chairman of the House Committee on Appropriations, under date of March 15, Secretary Wilson treats of this question further, and later Professor Galloway uses the same identical language in addressing Representative Candler, of Mississippi. The Secretary says:

As to the value of this miscellaneous distribution of garden and flower seeds. It is very difficult to state what it may be. There is little doubt in my mind. that such distribution accomplishes more or less good. Very few reports are received, however, and in the nature of the case it is impossible for us to use any but standard varieties in the distribution, because the quantities required make it impossible to use the rarer sorts. When this distribution was first undertaken, a great many years ago, there is no doubt that it accomplished much good, because at that time the seed industry was not as thoroughly organized as it is to-day. The practice of ordering through the mails from seed catalogues was not then in vogue, and it was extremely difficult for persons living in isolated localities to secure good garden seeds. This condition has changed, however, and to-day it is quite possible for anyone to buy garden seeds of the same varieties as we distribute.

Will any gentleman tell us how the distribution of turnip, radish, squash, and watermelon seed of the commonest varieties—Mr. Chairman, 690,000 pounds, 345 tons of it, cost only $90,000, an average of about 14 cents a pound—distributed in packets, of which it takes sometimes 120 to make a pound—how that is going to promote an industry whose yearly products run into the billions of dollars. Why, the contention is absurd.

Mr. Chairman, the distribution is well known to be in violation of law. Secretary Wilson admits it, but announces it is impossible to keep within the meaning of the original statute. The report of the Committee on Agriculture of the House of Representatives on the pending bill says:

There is not, and never has been, any warrant of law for this expenditure. The item has simply been tolerated in appropriation bills.

You are all familiar with the law on this subject, but, as all we are contending for is that Congress will abide by the law, we quote it: It reads as follows:

The purchase and distribution of seeds by the Department of Agriculture shall be confined to such seeds as are rare and uncommon to the country, to such as can be made more profitable by frequent changes from one part of the country to another, and the purchase, propagation, and distribution of trees, plants, shrubs, vines, and cuttings, shall be confined to such as are adapted to general cultivation, and to promote the general interests of horticulture and agriculture throughout the United States.

Now, Mr. Chairman, to that statute the seed trade has no objection whatever. Everyone recognizes the great good which has been accomplished by the Department of Agriculture through its scientists. The statute says, " and to procure, propagate, and distribute among the people new and valuable seeds and plants." Not a word about peas and beans and corn and tomato seeds of common varieties, nor, I may add, not a word about morning-glories or nasturtiums or four-o'clocks. Mr. Chairman, let us get back to the original meaning of the act—let us have the lucious pomegranate, the seedless orange, the seedless grape fruit, lychee nuts from China, and the lemon from Sicily; teach us, if you can, to raise the iceberg in the sunny South and to produce cotton in the Nevada mountains; give us a tobacco plant without nicotine, the fragrant Habana from Pennsylvania or Texas and the Sumatra from Florida and Connecticut. Employ Wizard Burbank, if you will, and import seed from every country and every clime. But do not waste public money and interfere with a legitimate business by distributing squash and parsnip seed.

I desire to have a statement of the cost of the distribution of seeds and table of appropriations inserted as a part of this hearing.

COST OF FREE DISTRIBUTION OF SEEDS, WITH TABLE SHOWING APPRO-
PRIATIONS BY YEARS.

*Memorandum of expenditures from the appropriation for the purchase and dis-
tribution of valuable seeds, 1906, as shown by financial statements to March
12, and estimates to June 30, 1906.*

1. THE SECURING, HANDLING, AND DISTRIBUTION OF MISCELLANEOUS GARDEN AND
FLOWER SEEDS, ETC.

Cost of seed:
Congressional vegetable and flower seed only_____ $63,072.67
Other seeds and plants entering into regular quotas, such as cot-
ton, tobacco, lawn grass, etc_____ 6,915.00
Seeds and orange trees not in regular quotas, but purchased for
distribution through Congressmen_____ 3,685.00
Plants, chiefly ornamentals, not in regular quotas, but to be dis-
tributed through Congressmen_____ 5,704.50

Total _____ 79,377.17

Contract for all work connected with the packeting and mailing of
35,815,000 packets of miscellaneous vegetable and flower seeds, including making the packets, printing and filling same, putting on
franks, assembling, and filling packages with packets, at contract
price of $1 per 1,000 packets_____ 36,000.00
Salaries of superintendent, bookkeepers, and frank counters_____ 7,645.33
Trial grounds, to test and determine the quality of seeds_____ 2,540.00
Miscellaneous, including freight on all seeds, rent, telegraph, telephone, gas and electric lighting, fuel, etc_____ 7,192.23

Total _____ 132,754.73

2. THE SECURING AND DISTRIBUTING OF COMPARATIVELY NEW OR LITTLE-KNOWN
KINDS OF VARIOUS FIELD AND FORAGE CROP SEEDS AND THE IMPROVEMENT OF
SAME BY BREEDING.

Purchase of seeds, expense of experimental work, including travel
for inspection and supervision_____ $18,450.33
Maintenance of propagating houses, trial grounds, cooperative work
with State experiment stations and private growers throughout
the country in establishing new plant industries, and necessary
expenses connected therewith of a miscellaneous character_____ 11,049.00
Salaries:
Botanist in charge of entire seed work and assistants _____ $9,272.17
Experts and laborers required in connection with
seeds and plants for experimental work_____ 8,419.67
Experts and gardeners for propagating work, trial
grounds, and cooperative investigations_____ 8,306.00
                                                                    25,997.84
Miscellaneous, including fuel, gas, and electric lighting, stationery,
and general office expenses_____ 10,394.33
Balance, not allotted to date, but will probably be required to meet
unforeseen expenses before the end of the fiscal year_____ 6,493.77

Total _____ 72,385.27

Total domestic seed work_____ 205,140.00

3. THE INTRODUCTION AND DISSEMINATION OF NEW AND PROMISING SEEDS AND PLANTS FROM FOREIGN COUNTRIES.

Purchase of seeds and plants in foreign countries, including travel expenses of explorers and special agents in connection therewith.	$16, 312. 31
Salaries of explorers, experts, special agents, clerks, and laborers in connection with foreign introductions	13, 049. 00
Preliminary tests of foreign introductions in cooperation with State experiment stations and private growers	3, 176. 00
Miscellaneous, including telegraph, express, storage, packing, etc	1, 000. 00
Balance not yet specifically allotted, but which will probably be required for unforeseen expenses	4, 242. 69
Total foreign seed introductions	37, 780. 00
Total appropriation for seed and plant introduction and distribution	242, 920. 00

Summary of principal items of interest.

	Amount.	Per cent of total.
Cost of seeds and plants, including freight	$118,767. 16	48.8
Packeting, assembling, and mailing under contract	36,000.00	14.8
Salaries: Botanist in charge, explorers, experts, special agents, clerks, gardeners, laborers, messengers, etc	46,692.17	19.2
Testing, trial grounds, cooperative tests of new plants with experiment stations and private growers, including travel expenses	16,765.00	6.9
Miscellaneous, including telegraph, telephone, fuel, gas and electric lighting, stationery, and general office expenses	13,959.21	5.8
Balance yet to be allotted	10,736.46	4.5
Total	242,920.00	100.0

From the foregoing it will be seen that approximately 49 per cent of the total appropriation is actually expended for the purchase of seeds, 15 per cent for packeting and mailing, 19 per cent for salaries, 7 per cent for testing and trial work, and 6 per cent for miscellaneous and office expenses, leaving a balance of 4 per cent for emergencies. The combined cost of all salaries, miscellaneous and general office expenses, including telegraph, amounts to $60,651.88, or approximately 25 per cent of the total, leaving $182,268.12, or 75 per cent of the entire appropriation as the net amount to be expended for the purchase of seeds, testing, and distribution.

In addition to the foregoing, attention should be called to the appropriation for salaries on the statutory roll of the Bureau of Plant Industry (Estimates of Appropriations, 1907, p. 87). The entire appropriation under this item is $162,480, of which $42,040, or approximately 25 per cent, is chargeable to the seed work. These salaries were formerly paid from the lump fund, but last year the Committee on Agriculture decided to make them statutory. Following is a list of all these clerks, together with their salaries and the line of work to which they are directly chargeable:

1. The securing, handling, and distribution of miscellaneous garden and flower seeds, etc.

Designation.	Number.	Rate.	Amount.
Clerks:			
Class 4	2	$1,800.00	$3,600.00
Class 3	8	1,600.00	1,600.00
Class 2		1,400.00	1,400.00
Class 1		1,200.00	2,400.00
Clerks		1,000.00	3,000.00
Clerk		840.00	840.00
Clerks		720.00	3,600.00
Clerk		600.00	600.00
Plant packer		660.00	660.00
Skilled laborer		660.00	660.00
Messengers		480.00	960.00
Total	20		19,320.00

2. The securing and distributing of comparatively new or little known kinds of various field and forage crop seeds and the improvement of same by breeding.

Designation.	Number.	Rate.	Amount.
Clerks:			
Class 2	1	$1,400.00	$1,400.00
Class 1	3	1,200.00	3,600.00
Clerks	2	1,000.00	2,000.00
Clerk	1	900.00	900.00
Clerks	3	840.00	2,520.00
Do	5	720.00	3,600.00
Clerk	1	600.00	600.00
Gardener	1	900.00	900.00
Do	1	600.00	600.00
Skilled laborer	1	660.00	660.00
Skilled laborers	4	600.00	2,400.00
Messenger boy	1	360.00	360.00
Total	24		19,540.00

3. The introduction and dissemination of new and promising seeds and plants from foreign countries.

Designation.	Number.	Rate.	Amount.
Clerk, class 1	1	$1,200.00	$1,200.00
Clerk	1	720.00	720.00
Gardener	1	660.00	660.00
Skilled laborer	1	600.00	600.00
Total	4		3,180.00

Total statutory salaries connected with seed work $42,040.00

From the foregoing it appears that the total cost of the seed work, including the regular appropriation and the amount expended for statutory salaries, is $284,960, or $5,040 less than the amount appropriated for the same purpose last year. The combined lump fund and statutory salaries this year amount to $88,732.17, or approximately 31 per cent of the entire cost of the seed work.

To properly handle such subjects we have a number of testing stations where crops when first brought in are grown for a time, and if found valuable are propagated extensively and distributed. The men in charge of these stations must be experts and must be thoroughly familiar with the propagation of plants and the necessary requirements for making such plants successful in other regions.

This statement in reference to the manner in which the work is handled seems desirable and necessary in order that a better understanding may be had of the accompanying summarized table of expenditures.

Very respectfully,   JAMES WILSON, *Secretary.*

Appropriations, purchase, and distribution of seeds from 1865 to 1905, inclusive.

Year.	Appropriated.	Expended.	Year.	Appropriated.	Expended.
1865	$61,000.00	$61,000.00	1887	$100,000.00	$99,998.87
1866	70,165.90	70,165.90	1888	103,000.00	102,587.55
1867	115,200.00	115,200.00	1889	104,200.00	104,168.73
1868	85,200.00	85,200.00	1890	104,200.00	104,174.55
1869	20,000.00	20,000.00	1891	105,400.00	105,090.94
1870	20,000.00	18,981.33	1892	150,000.00	(a)
1871	30,000.00	28,865.17	1892	105,400.00	104,920.35
1872	45,000.00	45,000.00	1893	135,400.00	134,908.27
1873	55,000.00	55,000.00	1894	135,400.00	119,719.76
1874	65,000.00	64,904.89	1895	165,400.00	120,545.15
1875	95,000.00	94,719.83	1896	135,400.00	126,476.87
1876	65,000.00	65,000.00	1897	150,000.00	142,822.52
1877	85,000.00	80,000.00	1898	130,000.00	121,870.38
1878	75,000.00	74,579.33	1899	130,000.00	127,150.52
1879	75,000.00	75,000.00	1900	130,000.00	118,561.53
1880	75,000.00	75,000.00	1901	170,000.00	149,615.49
1881	102,160.31	102,157.48	1902	270,000.00	266,614.12
1882	100,000.00	99,991.53	1903	270,000.00	253,133.70
1883	80,000.00	80,000.00	1904	290,000.00	284,254.21
1884	75,000.00	74,986.48	1905	290,000.00	280,530.30
1885	100,000.00	99,983.82			
1886	100,000.00	99,980.24	Total	4,767,526.21	

a For drought sufferers. Not used.

STATEMENT OF J. B. AGER, MASTER OF MARYLAND STATE GRANGE.

Mr. AGER. Mr. Chairman, during the hearing I received the impression that the questions asked by the Senators were: First, do the farmers desire the distribution of free seeds by their Congressmen, and, second, are they in favor of a small appropriation by the Government to obtain new and rare seeds and plants for them?

In reply to the first question I will say that I have been a farmer and dairyman all my life, and passed the three-score and ten milestone several years ago. For the past nine years I have been master of the Maryland State Grange, which is composed of a State grange, five Pomona or county granges, and sixty local or subordinate granges, with a membership of some 3,000. The question of the distribution of free seeds by the Government has been frequently discussed by our State, county, and subordinate granges, and numerous resolutions have been passed, demanding that the free distribution of the common varieties of field and garden seeds should be abandoned.

I have lived near Washington for the past twenty-seven years, have been well acquainted with some of the officials of the Department of Agriculture, and have seen the large force engaged in the seed division, and have learned of the enormous cost to the Government and of the very little benefit derived by the farmers. I have been receiving packages of seeds for thirty or more years, and for many years used to plant them with great care, thinking that they were some new variety, as I was requested to report my success to the Department. After repeated trials I found that they were only the common varieties, and often very common at that, and for several years past have not planted them. They lie about the house until my wife either feeds them to the chickens or burns them up. I think a better way would be not to receive them from the office or return them to the sender; then perhaps we might convince the Congressmen that we do not want them. I have frequently inquired of gardeners and truckers, as they are called, about Washington, and they invariably tell me that they would not take the seeds from the Department if they could have all they wanted without cost, as they would rather go to a reliable dealer and pay for them; then if they did not prove to be true to name they would have some one to fall back on.

After learning the feeling of the gardeners and farmers composing our organization in Maryland, we desired to know if the same feeling existed in other States; so at the session of the National Grange held at Portland, Oreg., in November, 1904, I introduced a resolution referred to by Ex-Governor Bachelder in his address before your committee. The resolution was referred to the committee on agriculture of the National Grange, and they reported that the free distribution of seeds by the Department should be abandoned. There were 27 States and 800,000 farmers represented, and the report of the committee was adopted without a dissenting vote.

Since then many of the States have adopted similar resolutions, notably the State of New York at their late session held at Geneva, representing 70,000 members.

In reply to the second question, as to whether the grangers and farmers would recommend an appropriation of $40,000 for the purchase by the Department of some new and rare plants, grains, fruits, and vegetables, I should say that they would recommend it provided they were sent to the several experiment stations, and if found to be adapted to our soil and climatic conditions, and of any value, to be distributed from there. We believe that $300,000 could be expended in other ways to promote agriculture which would benefit the farmers and the whole country more than in sending him a 5-cent package of seeds. What we farmers most need is a better agricultural education. We want to know as dairymen how to feed our cows a well-balanced ration to produce the best results, and how to feed our land so as to cause two blades of grass to grow where one grew before.

The Department of Agriculture, the agricultural experiment stations, the grange farm institutes, and the agricultural press are doing a grand work for the education of the farmer; and the prosperity of the farmers, which means the prosperity of all other classes, for the last decade we attribute to this education. We have, as an illustration, the instruction of Professor Holden on corn growing to the farmers of Iowa, which has raised the yield from 27 bushels per acre to 40 bushels in the last three years, and he states that every ounce we can add to the standard ear of corn, which is about 9 or 10 ounces, will add $9,000,000 to the farmers of the State. Now, the money expended in bringing about such results would benefit the farmer and country at large more than in sending him a 5-cent package of garden seeds. We sincerely hope that you will not concur in the House bill, but will cut the appropriation down to what was recommended by the House committee ($40,000) and give the balance for the promotion of agriculture in some other way.

The CHAIRMAN. The chairman of this committee has received a number of communications from newspapers, societies, and various people protesting against the present practice of the free distribution of seeds, and I will submit brief extracts from some of those received.

NASHVILLE, TENN., *May 8, 1906.*

Senator REDFIELD PROCTOR,
    Chairman Senate Committee on Agriculture, Washington, D. C.

DEAR SIR: As a letter from the Southern Agriculturist figured rather prominently in the discussion of the subject of free seeds in a debate in the House recently, and as the same subject, we understand, is to come before your committee shortly, we take occasion to make very plain our views on the subject.

In the first place, we do not seek or favor a reduction of the appropriation for the Agricultural Department. All that we have expressed a wish for is that the money which is now expended for the purchase of ordinary garden and field seeds to be distributed by Congressmen among their rural constituents be used strictly for the purpose for which the appropriation was originally intended, as the Department of Agriculture has done a great deal in developing new varieties and discovering rare seeds and making them common to the average farmer. If the appropriation in question were used for a similar purpose, we believe it would work greatly to the benefit of the farming class.

We know, however, from frequent and long-extended contact with farmers in this and other States that the free distribution as now conducted is looked on as a sort of political graft, and we do not believe that one-tenth of the seeds so distributed are used in an appreciative way. The least objection we have to the free-seed distribution is that it simply gives to the farmer who does use them something that he could buy in any country store, and thus comes in competition with a legitimate line of trade.

As the charge was openly made on the floor of the House that the attitude of this paper and others of its class was traceable to the large amount of seed advertising that we carry, we will state that not as much as 10 per cent of our total receipts from advertising come from seed announcements, and that of this 10 per cent a large proportion comes from farmers who are advertising the seeds which they raise themselves. We know, as a matter of fact, that there is an organization of seed dealers which is endeavoring to put a stop to this free distribution, but the suggestion that their advertising has anything to do with the attitude of the agricultural press is as absurd as it is unjust.

In conclusion, we beg to say that we believe that our attitude on this subject is seconded by practically every daily paper of importance in the South, and we know that the better class of farmers are with us.

Trusting that this letter may furnish some information that will be useful in the deliberations of your committee, we are,

Yours, very truly,

SOUTHERN AGRICULTURIST CO.

EXTRACTS FROM LETTERS RECEIVED FROM PUBLISHERS.

The New England Farmer, Brattleboro, Vt.—Wish to protest against the continuation of this pernicious practice.

The American Cultivator, Boston, Mass.—It seems a form of graft, the same in principle as that often seen on a larger scale in public affairs.

The Connecticut Farmer.—We strongly protest against the passage of the "free seed" appropriation. The sentiment of the farming interests of Connecticut are strongly opposed to this species of graft.

Farm and Fireside, Springfield, Ohio.—For many years past have steadfastly opposed the free distribution of common garden and flower seeds. During that time the contributors and readers, as far as known, have approved of the stand taken. Expressions of their opinion have been in favor of it. In fact, not one expressed a desire to have Congressional free-seed distribution continued.

The American Stock Farm, Winona, Minn.—Are opposed to free distribution of seeds. The present plan is a farce that does not even influence votes, but wastes a lot of public money, and the sooner it is discontinued the better for all concerned.

Daily Eagle-Star, Marinette, Wis.—It has been represented to us that newspapers were opposing a free-seed distribution because of the amount of advertising received from wholesale dealers. So far as we are concerned, and we believe that what we say of ourselves is true of newspapers generally, no such idea influences our opposition to this distribution. Our foreign advertising probably runs about $3,000 per year, but of this there is scarcely $25 that can be traced to seed matters in any form. We are opposed on general principles, because we believe it would be a burden to the mails, and that it creates a deficit in the Post-Office Department which must be made up by other industries, or be a charge against the Department not provided for.

The Southern Farm Gazette, Starkville, Miss.—Trust your committee will do nothing to perpetuate the fraud that is being perpetrated on the American people through the free distribution of seeds on the present basis. Know of a number of instances in which people who never plant a seed receiving packages and throwing them away or using them for poultry feed.

The Progressive Farmer, Raleigh, N. C.—There is still a chance for the Senate to redeem Congress from the disgrace of the free-seed graft. Hope that your committee will be able to defeat this fraud.

Farmers' Tribune, Sioux City, Iowa.—The Tribune represents 45,000 farmers, and in behalf of our constituency we trust the distribution of free seeds by the Government may soon be terminated.

Wallace's Farmer, Des Moines, Iowa.—Wallace's Farmer has for years looked upon this free-seed distribution as a humbug which ought to be discontinued.

The Oklahoma Farm Journal, Oklahoma City, Okla.—The Journal objects to this distribution.

Minnesota Daily News, Minneapolis, Minn.—The opposition of the Daily News of Minneapolis to distribution of free seeds is not due to any advertising influence. It is absurd to think that the amount of advertising which we secure from seed houses should influence our editorial columns.

The Gleaner, Detroit, Mich.—It is not from a selfish standpoint that this publication has opposed the giving away of seeds. Think the time was when the farmer appreciated the gift and it no doubt did much good, but at the present time when a farmer receives seeds from a Congressman, in nine times out of ten the remark is made that he is after a vote.

The Practical Farmer, Philadelphia, Pa.—The whole thing is pure, petty graft, and it is to be hoped the Senate will right the wrong. While the seedsmen of the country certainly have good reason to complain of an interference with their business which is not done with any other business, the real objection is that the whole thing is a robbery of the many for slight benefit to few and is class legislation of the most vicious sort.

The Rural New Yorker, New York City.—Respectfully enter protest against the continuance of the free-seed distribution. By holding back this appropriation and cutting off the seed distribution the Senate will appeal to the better sentiment of our best farmers.

The Ohio Farmer, Cleveland, Ohio.—We are pretty close to the agricultural public, and it is not considered at all an important or needed measure by the farmers of the United States. We have opposed this use of the public funds for years.

The Bee Publishing Company, Omaha, Nebr.—Wish to register a protest against the continuance of the free distribution of the common garden seeds by Congress. Editorially the Omaha Daily Bee and the Twentieth Century Farmer have condemned this needless expenditure of money.

The Wisconsin Agriculturist, Racine, Wis.—Desire to say most earnestly that from personal knowledge of the value of free-seed distribution such appropriation should not be allowed.

Farm, Stock, and Home, Minneapolis, Minn.—We are both surprised and disappointed to see that the free-seed graft has passed the House. Sincerely hope the Senate will defeat the bill.

The Strawberry, Three Rivers, Mich.—Hope that your committee will see to it that the recent action of the House on the matter of free seed be not approved by the Senate.

Topeka Daily Capital.—The sentiment of this State is overwhelmingly for the discontinuance of this graft.

The Prairie Farmer, Chicago, Ill.—We have been somewhat surprised to notice that even after the Committee on Agriculture condemned the free distribution of home garden seeds that the House has deliberately reinstated section. Hope you will endeavor to eliminate same from bill that is to be passed by Senate.

PROTESTS AGAINST DISTRIBUTION OF FREE SEED.

I desire to file a protest, both officially and personally, against this expensive folly and petty graft.—(*W. N. Giles, secretary New York State Grange.*)

We desire to be placed on record as being opposed to the free distribution of seeds.—(*Olive Branch Grange, No. 142, Matawan, N. J.*)

We deem the free distribution of Government seed to be a needless expense and burden to the country without adequate return.—(*Bear Hill Grange, No. 39, Henniker, N. H.*)

We call upon Congress to abolish its petty, annoying, and needless practice of broadcasting free and common garden seeds all over the rural districts, and that the control of seed distribution be placed under the Department of Agriculture and limited to experimental work.—(*State Grange of Illinois.*)

We respectfully urge upon our Representatives in Congress and the United States Senators from New York that they use their best efforts to have this practice stopped. We denounce it as a useless waste of public money and a flagrant perversion of the aims and intent of the law creating the Department of Agriculture.—(*The Horticultural Society of New York.*)

If the Government has any new or rare seeds that should be sent out for testing, that is all right, and the horticulturists of Minnesota would like to get their share of such kinds, but we have no use for a free distribution of ordinary garden seeds such as every seedsman handles.—(*A. W. Latham, secretary Minnesota State Horticultural Society.*)

I regard it as a useless expenditure of money. It would be far better to buy up new agricultural products of value and distribute them among the experiment stations. * * * I am engaged in horticulture, but not in the seed trade.—(*N. B. White, Norwood, Mass.*)

Professor Taft and myself stand against the free distribution of seed by the great Department at Washington.—(*C. D. Smith, director Michigan Experiment Station.*)

In the prosecution of my work it is my privilege to meet a good many bodies of agricultural men, and I find an almost universal condemnation of the free-seed appropriation as it is now administered.—(*W. H. Jordan, director New York Agricultural Experiment Station.*)

AGRICULTURAL COLLEGES.

STATEMENT OF DR. H. C. WHITE, OF THE UNIVERSITY OF GEORGIA.

Doctor WHITE. Mr. Chairman, I thank you very much for permitting me to appear before this committee. I may introduce myself by saying that I occupy the position of president of the College of Agriculture, University of Georgia, and am the director of its experiment station. The agricultural colleges and experiment stations of the United States, as is well known, have a national organization, and they meet together annually for the discussion of matters in which they are mutually interested. For the conduct of their business they appoint an executive committee, and I am chairman of that executive committee and have been for several years. Therefore I think I know the attitude of the members of the association toward matters which are presented to the committee. Moreover, they have also taken action from time to time in their annual conventions, and by resolution and otherwise, so I think I speak with authority in saying what I am going to say.

There are two or three matters which will be presented to the consideration of this committee in connection with the agricultural appropriation bill, in which we are interested. First, we have endeavored for a number of years in our association, and by individual effort on the part of the college men, to systematize agricultural education. That has been an extremely difficult task. When these agricultural colleges were founded, we found that education in mathematics, for example, and in English, and even in the pure sciences, had been systematized for a number of years, and had assumed what Doctor Harris, Commissioner of Education, calls a pedagogic form. There was no difficulty in teaching those things, for they had been taught for years and some of them for centuries. But education in agriculture was a new thing.

We have endeavored faithfully for a number of years to beat out courses in agriculture which will have the same educational value as the courses in the pure sciences, in mathematics, in English, or any other of the well-known pedagogics of our institutions. I think we have succeeded fairly well, so far as college education is concerned; and if you gentlemen should go to any of those large institutions—such as the ones in Illinois, New York, Wisconsin, and elsewhere—would find that those immense establishments, utilizing fields, stables, dairies, and all those things, have applied in their educational work just those courses which have come finally to be mapped out by the committees of this association. But we find a difficulty in doing the work that we would like to do in colleges, because the schools do not give the preparation for entrance into those technical courses in agriculture that they do in other courses in a college or university. So, for the last two or three years, we have undertaken to work a little further back, a little lower down, in trying to map out courses of instruction in the schools, and we hope ultimately to carry it back into the most elementary schools, so that the child, when he first goes to school, shall be taken in hand in part by men who are in sympathy with and who are learned in this kind of technical instruction that we are giving in colleges, so that there may be some degree of preparation for the children when they come to college.

Now that is, of course, a right big proposition to undertake, but we are endeavoring to start about it in a right way, and we have found a very great deal of value in work of the experiment stations of the Department of Agriculture, in getting together information for us which we, perhaps, could not get individually ourselves. They have an organization there that is in touch with every State in the Union, and with foreign countries. They have their correspondents, and they can get the courses of study, and all that sort of thing, in every State and in other countries and bring it together, in that way assembling an immense mass of information which individuals or even individual institutions could not do with the same facility.

Now, we have asked the Secretary of Agriculture, therefore, if he would not extend the work of that office. We have already provided for these farmers' institutes, and there is what is called a clearing house of farmers' institutes. We have asked the Secretary if he could not extend the work of that office, so as to aid us in this matter, and he said that he could, and all he needed was more money. I do not know the amount, but I think it is something like five or six thousand dollars that has been asked for. I really have not informed myself on that, because we would rather leave with the Secretary the question of the amount; but what I wanted to make plain to this committee, if I might be permitted, was the fact that the colleges of the country are in sympathy with that movement, and I know that it has arisen, in large degree, out of their initiative. They think that work of that sort, done in the Department of Agriculture, in the office of the experiment stations, would be of immense value to them. How much it would cost, the Secretary can tell much better than we can. How far you gentlemen think it is compatible with governmental functions, is for you to determine. My duty is to make plain to you, if I can, that the colleges unanimously favor that proposition. They think it will be of advantage to them to have it.

Senator HANSBROUGH. I did not catch your suggestion with respect to the method by which you proposed to begin with the elementary part of this transaction in the common schools, as I understand, among the children, so as to lay the basis for what you hope to accomplish later in the colleges. How could we reach that?

Doctor WHITE. That is just what we do not know.

Senator PERKINS. I think we have given the Secretary all he estimated for in his book, have we not?

Doctor WHITE. I do not know about that.

Senator PERKINS. That is my impression. I know that the committee generally are in sympathy with the work in which you are engaged—the work of experimental stations.

The CHAIRMAN. We have not formally acted on it, but there has never been any objection to the appropriation.

Doctor WHITE. Are you quite sure of the amount? When we have any trouble with the House of Representatives we come to the Senate.

Senator HANSBROUGH. Aside from any question in regard to the amount, I am at a loss to know how we could apply an appropriation made by the National Government to instruction in the common schools.

Doctor WHITE. No, sir; you would not do that.

Senator HANSBROUGH. As we understand, you want to go back and begin these courses in the common schools.

Doctor WHITE. Yes; I will explain to you. What I meant to say was that our association, composed of teachers and educators, want to formulate courses of instruction that we may suggest to the schools. We do not want to undertake the giving of the instruction.

Senator HANSBROUGH. In the common schools?

Doctor WHITE. Yes.

Senator HANSBROUGH. Perhaps you mean by lectures from professors in the agricultural colleges.

Doctor WHITE. No, sir; not at all; but to formulate courses of study. We want to be able to tell them in the common schools what to do. Of course if I knew now, there would be no need of this work, but we do not know; but we think that there ought to be in the common schools some kind of instruction. An attempt is now made to give instruction in nature study, but that hardly goes far enough, in the estimation of most of us, and we think that by all working together we may formulate a course. Then we would say to the elementary schools: "We are not going to give this course, but you ought to teach this thing in the schools." We are not asking for any money to do that with. We want to make a study of the whole question, so that we may be able to advise the schools.

Senator HANSBROUGH. Can you not do that without requiring any additional appropriation here?

Doctor WHITE. It is possible, but the Secretary says not. He says, for example, that his Office of Experiment Stations has already all the work it can do; that it would require, perhaps, one man, a clerk, or something of that sort, just as in the case of the farmers' institute work when that was taken up; it required the appointment of one man. I really do not know whether the appointment of a new man would be necessary or not. We do not advocate any new office for anybody or anything of that sort.

Senator HANSBROUGH. But you propose to reach the elementary schools merely by way of suggestion.

Doctor WHITE. That is all, sir.

Senator HANSBROUGH. From the experiment stations?

Doctor WHITE. From the colleges.

Senator PERKINS. They would be obliged to formulate a course of study and prepare text-books, I suppose.

Doctor WHITE. That would lead to that, but anything involving any large expense is not in our contemplation here at all; but all we ask is that, as the Secretary has assented to that, your committee may consider favorably any proposition which will enable the experiment station to act as a clearing house, as we call it, for the work of this association. Now, I was informed that the appropriation act as it came from the House eliminated something of that sort. I am not sure about that.

The CHAIRMAN. I did not see the estimate.

Senator PERKINS. Here it is.

An increase in the appropriation for the formation of farmers' institutes and agricultural schools is recommended to enable the Department to extend its work of aiding in the diffusion of agricultural information and education among the masses of farmers and their children, in cooperation with the State authorities in charge of farmers' institutes and agricultural schools; and the changes suggested in the language of the appropriation act are intended to aid the Department's work in relation to farmers' institutes in connection with the schools.

The CHAIRMAN. He has asked for an increase of about $13,000.

Doctor WHITE. I think an increase of $8,000.

The CHAIRMAN. Bringing the appropriation up to the full amount of the estimate, $812,600. There is also a specification that $43,000 of that shall be expended in the Territories of Alaska, Hawaii, and Porto Rico.

Doctor WHITE. Yes. What Senator Perkins has read is exactly the point. I see an increase in the appropriation is asked for. I did not know how much that was.

The CHAIRMAN. That is not a large increase. I am inclined to think the committee will look favorably upon giving the Department what they ask for.

Doctor WHITE. That was all. We understood the Department had asked for it.

The CHAIRMAN. Now, Doctor White, we have had a hearing this morning in regard to this seed distribution. You were present during some of this hearing. We feel that you are in a position where you would know the intelligent opinion of southern people, and that you are also disinterested, of course being interested merely for the general good of agriculture. What do you say about the present form of seed distribution, whether it is a good use of the money?

Doctor WHITE. Of course I think my individual judgment was made up long years ago, that the Government might put that money to much better use than in the distribution of the seeds. Now, I try to maintain that as an individual opinion.

Senator PERKINS. It is based upon your observation and your connection with the work with which you are engaged and intercourse with the farmers of the country?

Doctor WHITE. This is rather a delicate matter, but I believe if you take the intelligent farmers of the State—they are almost unanimously either in opposition to the free distribution of seeds, or certainly they would not advocate it. Now, if I were to make that statement publicly, it might stand as a reflection upon the intelligence of a great many farmers, and I would not like to do that. There are a great many men who can not be called unintelligent, and who yet hear nothing one way or the other on this subject. I do not doubt that there are a great many people who work small farms, and all that sort of thing, who would apply for free seeds if they were to be had; but if you come to the sound public intelligent opinion on the subject, I am quite prepared to say that it is as strong in Georgia as it is in any other State, and that they would be glad to see the free-seed distribution done away.

Senator HANSBROUGH. I have found a new demand for these Government seeds, which rather commends itself to me. That is from the school-teachers throughout my State. They are writing to this effect: " We would be glad to have as many garden and flower seeds as you can spare, so that we may have an experimental garden, in which we can employ the time of the children."

Doctor WHITE. Yes; I think that is true, and I think that would be a judicious distribution.

Senator HANSBROUGH. I sent to the county superintendents of

schools in several counties of my State large packages of seeds, and they have distributed them in all the schoolhouses in those counties, and the teachers have distributed them among the children, and they have been planting experimental gardens, and in one place I had some pictures sent to me of about 25 children out in a little field working with hoes.

Doctor WHITE. We have done that.

Senator HANSBROUGH. That rather commends itself to me.

Doctor WHITE. It does to me absolutely; but you observe that is a different proposition. That is a distribution of seed for the benefit of education, and we advocate that, and we are trying to get school gardens in every rural school in the State, and flower beds, and so on; and we have always told them that they could apply to the Department of Agriculture and get seeds. Now, distribution of that sort, of course, is a different proposition from the distribution to an individual; and the latter, I am quite sure, does not commend itself to a great many people.

The CHAIRMAN. Could not that distribution to schools be made through the experiment stations?

Doctor WHITE. That is where it should be, through the experiment station or college, or some central establishment, and they are generally located together.

Senator HANSBROUGH. I should say you would have to authorize it by some legislation.

Doctor WHITE. What I mean to say is that if the Secretary of Agriculture were empowered to make this distribution of the seeds, to give so many to each State and to distribute them through the experiment stations——

Senator HANSBROUGH. You would have to specify the purpose for which they were to be distributed.

Doctor WHITE. That certainly would relieve the distribution of one serious embarrassment to which Congressional distribution now subjects it.

There was one other matter in which we are interested. That is the matter of human nutrition. The House, on a point of order, struck out that entire section, which had been carried in the agricultural appropriation bill for a good many years, making provision for investigations in human nutrition in the Department of Agriculture.

Senator HANSBROUGH. Is that the business that is going on under Doctor Wiley?

Doctor WHITE. Oh, no; it is a new scientific study of human nutrition. It bears upon our work in home economics. The women are more interested in it than the men. Our teachers almost universally use the literature of the Department of Agriculture, from that bureau, in their instruction work. We think that if it be discontinued it would be rather unfortunate.

Senator HANSBROUGH. Did that go out on a point of order in the House?

Doctor WHITE. It went out on a point of order in the House.

Senator HANSBROUGH. I think it is a very important matter.

The CHAIRMAN. It will not be subject to a point of order in the Senate.

Senator HANSBROUGH. I want to know how much nutrition there is in the food I eat.

Doctor WHITE. We use the facts that they obtain in our instruction work. I merely wanted to say that we are much interested in that, and if it is of any value to them we want to put it on record.

Thereupon the committee adjourned.

<hr>

COMMITTEE ON AGRICULTURE AND FORESTRY,
UNITED STATES SENATE,
Washington, D. C., Tuesday, May 15, 1906.

The committee met at 10.30 o'clock a. m.

Present: Senators Proctor (chairman), Hansbrough, Dolliver, Burnham, Long, Simmons, Latimer, and Frazier.

INVESTIGATION OF ADULTERATION OF FOODS, ETC.

STATEMENT OF J. A. YERINGTON, ESQ.

Senator LATIMER. What is your position?

Mr. YERINGTON. I am the chairman of the board of directors of what is known as the National Food Manufacturers' Association. It was through the action of that association that we had introduced in the Senate what was known as the Money amendment to Senate bill 88, introduced by Senator Money.

Senator LATIMER. That is, to the pure-food bill?

Mr. YERINGTON. To the pure-food bill. I will state that the object in having that amendment introduced as it was, as an amendment to that bill, was because we endeavored to have a hearing, and expected to have one, before the Committee on Manufactures of the Senate, and on the 8th of December the bill was introduced by Senator Heyburn, the chairman of the committee, referred to that committee, and reported back favorably to the Senate on the 14th of the same month, or about six days afterwards, which eliminated the manufacturers from having the hearing that they anticipated. I wrote, some time previous to that, stating that we were coming here with a bill that clearly defined and set forth the views of the manufacturers in regard to a pure-food bill, and with the request or the understanding that we should have a hearing. Upon consulting many of the Senators afterwards, they thought it was better to have that introduced as a substitute, so that it could be printed and placed before the members of the Senate, so that during the discussion of the pure-food bill the views of the manufacturers would undoubtedly be taken up at the same time, and we thought that probably there would be many points in our bill that would assist the Senators in formally passing a pure-food bill.

We made the same request of Chairman Hepburn, of the House committee, and he replied to me and told me to come here and bring the bill and have it introduced, and it would receive consideration. We did, and had Mr. Rodenberg introduce the bill at the same time on the floor of the House, and we had our hearings before the Interstate Commerce Committee on the pure-food question. The manufacturers were here, and their chemists, and all of that, and had their hearing.

The CHAIRMAN. Those hearings will be printed, will they not?

Mr. YERINGTON. They have been printed.

The CHAIRMAN. We have access to them, then?

Mr. YERINGTON. You have access to them.

The CHAIRMAN. So that it will not be necessary for us to go over that ground.

Mr. YERINGTON. It will not be necessary to go into that matter at the present time. I simply want to take the opportunity, which we have never had, as far as the Senate is concerned, of defining our position.

The statement went abroad that the manufacturers of the United States, of food products especially (I am speaking now as a member of this association), were coming here for the purpose of preventing, if possible, the passage of a pure-food bill. I would like to say, Senator, that that is entirely erroneous. It was at the suggestion of the late Senator Platt, of Connecticut, that this association was formed. During the debate a year ago on the floor of the Senate he repeatedly stated that the manufacturers of food products of the United States did not know themselves what they wanted, and that they had not expressed themselves as to what they wanted; and he suggested that the manufacturers get together and express their views in regard to a pure-food bill.

This association was subsequently formed upon that basis. We took great care in the preparation of our bill, and submitted it to ex-Senator Thurston and others, who passed upon its constitutionality. The bill received a great deal of publicity. We had it published in nearly all of the leading trade journals of the United States some six months before the convening of Congress, and endeavored to have everyone interested in the question lend as much aid as he could toward perfecting the bill. So that when we appeared here it was with the understanding that we had taken a great deal of time in preparing such a bill.

Then I afterwards had the honor to receive a letter in regard to our bill from one of the officials of Australia. The government of Australia at the present time is preparing a pure-food bill, and its officials were so much impressed with the comments upon the bill that they sent to me here and had me send them six copies of our bill, with the comments on it which we had published. We did that so as to make it very clear, and so that all the provisions of the bill would be thoroughly understood.

Senator LATIMER. Now, as I understand it, the provision which you object to has been stricken out of this bill in the House?

Mr. YERINGTON. It has been stricken out of the agricultural appropriation bill. I will state that I called a meeting of the leading manufacturers a few weeks ago at the Waldorf-Astoria. I think there were some forty-three of the representative packers and canners of the United States, members of our association, and other people present at that meeting. There were also present some chemists and newspaper men—that is, men connected with the trade journals. The consensus of opinion, as I stated in my letter to you, Senator, at that meeting was that we should have a pure-food bill pass Congress; and, as far as the members of our association are concerned, they are very desirous that it shall be done. The manufacturers to-day find themselves in such a position, owing to the conflicting State laws (which you gentlemen are undoubtedly posted on) in regard to labeling, and all of that, that they are being caused a great deal of uneasiness and put to a great deal of additional expense.

Senator LATIMER. What is the objection to that bill?

Mr. YERINGTON. The present objection to the bill is the fact that the Department of Agriculture insists upon maintaining the position it has assumed, owing to the power given to it through the rider that has passed on the appropriation bill in past years, as to the appointing of a standards committee for passing upon standards, and that the manufacturer has never as yet been able to have his day in court. That is, when the Government of the United States once placed its ban upon his goods, they were virtually condemned by the Government; and it was almost impossible for him to bring a suit and fight the fact and gain his justice, owing to the fact that he had already been turned down by the United States Government. I think that any man in that position finds it very difficult to bring a suit and take the matter through to the Supreme Court when he has to show that he has already been turned down by the Government.

Senator BURNHAM. The Government acts without any hearing?

Mr. YERINGTON. The Government acts without any hearing, and all the manufacturers asked for was their day in court.

Senator LATIMER. You refer to the branding of articles?

Mr. YERINGTON. Yes, sir. Take, for instance, the "poison squad" that Doctor Wiley had here in regard to the use of certain preservatives. He made his report to the Secretary of Agriculture that he had taken these young fellows and had been feeding them boracic acid, which he contended was injurious to health. That was known commonly all over the country as the "poison squad." That information was sent promiscuously all over the country as being authentic, although such chemists as Liebrich, of Germany, and other leading chemists in the United States thoroughly disagreed with Doctor Wiley, and especially with the course he pursued in arriving at the conclusion he did in regard to the injurious effect upon these men of having taken this boracic acid. There is a great contention about the matter and to-day it is an open question. I have had published, and had before the Committee on Interstate Commerce of the House, Liebrich's report, in German, but unfortunately I did not have an interpreter present.

Senator LATIMER. Let me suggest one point right there: As has been intimated, we have not a great deal of time; and this matter, as it seems to me, is not before this committee, because it is out of the bill unless we choose to reinsert it.

Mr. YERINGTON. It is at present entirely out of the bill.

Senator LATIMER. But the point I want to make with you is this: Under this pure-food bill, if on inspection it is found that an article contains substances that are injurious to health, and are so stated by Doctor Wiley or those who have charge of the matter, have not you an opportunity to be heard in connection with it—I mean to say under that bill?

Mr. YERINGTON. As the bill passed the Senate, in championing it, both Senators Heyburn and McCumber stated specifically that in no way would that bill recognize any standards; and to that end, therefore, it was not in any conflict with the police powers of the various States. The bill was amended and passed in the Senate, and, as the Congressional Record shows, there were debates upon it. Both of those Senators dwelt upon that very emphatically that there would be no "one man" power and no "one department" power in the bill; that the standards should simply be for the guidance of the courts, but that there should be no decisions rendered in any way by the Department of Agriculture, and therefore that the bill actually recognized no standards except those that had already been made by the various State food commissioners.

When the bill got over to the House it was completely amended, as you probably understand, from the enacting clause right through, and the House bill was substituted, together with numerous amendments. Since that time other amendments have been prepared by the subcommittee to be reported on the floor of the House.

Senator LATIMER. Then, as I gather, the bill as it passed the Senate is not objectionable to you?

Mr. YERINGTON. It was not objectionable.

Senator LATIMER. It is the House proposition that you object to?

Mr. YERINGTON. Of course, there were certain amendments which we still wanted to the Senate bill. There were quite a number. We saw defects, as we felt, in the bill in regard to its constitutionality.

Senator LATIMER. Did you have hearings before the House on that subject?

Mr. YERINGTON. We had hearings before the House, but of course we could not tell what action the committee would take; and when the bill came out from the House committee it came out virtually as a new bill. But we had the satisfaction of showing to the committee of the House how essential it was, in order to give the manufacturers a "square deal" and let them cooperate with the Department and do all they could, and in order that they should be represented, that a disinterested board of five chemists should be appointed to act in conjunction with the other two boards—that is, the State food commissioners and the Board of Standards.

Senator BURNHAM. Is any board provided for in the House bill?

Mr. YERINGTON. It is provided for in the House bill, and in the agricultural appropriation bill that matter was totally ignored; and we now have an amendment to that bill that I included in my letter of May 7 to Senator Proctor, your chairman.

Senator LATIMER. Mr. Chairman, it seems to me that if we are going to take up this question we ought to have a hearing, and that if we are going to hear one side we ought to have both sides present at the hearing when the committee is present. I do not see that we have a thing to do with that matter now. It is not in this bill at all.

Mr. YERINGTON. I am simply stating now the stand the manufacturers take in regard to having the point of order that was raised on the floor of the House eliminated, as it was, from the appropriation bill. They do not consider that that matter is pertinent to the appropriation bill; that the pure-food bill to-day is pending and——

The CHAIRMAN. That is the clause reading "To investigate the adulteration of foods, condiments," etc., is it?

Mr. YERINGTON. Yes; that is the clause.

The CHAIRMAN. It is on page 30.

Mr. YERINGTON. Now, this is the amendment that the manufacturers to-day want to offer to the pure-food bill on the floor of the House; and they will stand by the bill and will be perfectly satisfied if this is adopted. As the bill reads to-day, it simply states that the Secretary of Agriculture is authorized to call upon this committee as he sees fit; but they make it that—

> The Secretary of Agriculture shall call upon the committee on food standards of the Association of Official Agricultural Chemists and the committee on standards of the Association of State Dairy and Food Departments, and such other experts as he may deem necessary.

It formerly read: "And upon request made to the Secretary of Agriculture prior to reaching any decision as provided in this section," etc. They eliminate that and suggest the following:

> Upon request made to him by any manufacturer or other person interested asking for the appointment of a board to assist in determining all such matters concerning which the person making the request has an interest, it shall be the duty of the Secretary of Agriculture to appoint a board of disinterested experts, which board shall consist of five members, one of whom shall be an expert toxicologist, one an expert physiological chemist, one an expert bacteriologist, one an expert pathologist, and one an expert pharmacologist, none of whom shall in any way be connected with any department of the Government or State food or health departments——

Making it thoroughly a disinterested board.

> Which board shall meet at the city of Washington, District of Columbia, or elsewhere, at the call of the Secretary of Agriculture, and decide upon such questions, after proper notice and hearing granted to the person making such request. The compensation of the members of such board shall be fixed by the Secretary of Agriculture.

The CHAIRMAN. That is what you propose to offer in the House?

Mr. YERINGTON. In the House.

The CHAIRMAN. It is not anything that we have anything to do with yet?

Mr. YERINGTON. You have nothing to do with it yet; but I simply want to show this, Senator, that the provisions as made thoroughly eliminated this matter on the point of order. After having all of our hearings before that committee, and after that provision was embodied in the pure-food bill and your agricultural appropriation bill it was thoroughly eliminated.

Now, the manufacturers raise this point: If the two bills pass, which they both will—your appropriation bill and the pure-food bill—there is no question or doubt about it, which bill will the Secretary of Agriculture assume his power under? Will he exercise the power given to him by the agricultural appropriation bill or will he follow along these lines in the pure-food bill?

The CHAIRMAN. If he gets both he can take his choice, can he not?

Mr. YERINGTON. The manufacturers want to know that, and I think it is only due to them that they should, when you realize what this represents to them.

The CHAIRMAN. We are not considering the pure-food bill now, of course.

Mr. YERINGTON. No; I appreciate that. But the agricultural appropriation bill covered that point, and I want to appear before you, gentlemen, and bring this point before you as one reason why I consider that it should not be reinstated in this agricultural bill. Your pure-food bill to-day is almost ready; it is at such a stage now that it can be called up on the floor of the House at any time.

The CHAIRMAN. It seems to me that is hardly sound. We do not know whether there will be a pure-food bill or not. We are considering the agricultural bill and I do not know whether we will restore that clause now.

Mr. YERINGTON. Well, Senator, if your pure-food bill passes at this session I do not think this will be pertinent in the appropriation bill. If it does not pass, I can assure you gentlemen of one thing, and I think I can express the sentiment of three or four hundred of the leading manufacturers of the United States, that if this bill in conference should not be agreed upon and passed, the manufacturers will do all within their power before the next convening of Congress to come here and to take these bills that seemed objectionable and eliminate such portions of them that they will be in harmony, and they will render their assistance in that direction. They are anxious to have such a bill passed so that eventually the various States of the Union can have their laws to conform to one bill.

The CHAIRMAN. Suppose we should restore that item—we have not considered it, but suppose we should? The bill will have to pass the Senate and then go into conference. The conference can strike it out entirely. If the pure-food bill has a provision in it that supplants this one, or is better than this, the conference can strike it out. Our putting it in does not make it a law.

Mr. YERINGTON. Of course, if the manufacturers were assured to-day that that would be the case, they would feel very, very much easier. But I have been in receipt of hundreds and hundreds of telegrams and letters, from the Pacific to the Atlantic, urging me to appear before you gentlemen on this matter. It is a very, very grave question with them, and it is causing a great deal of disquiet in regard to their business. Many of the manufacturers to-day are really in such a position that they do not know what to do, or what will be the consequence of this agitation—whether this provision will be in the agricultural bill or whether it is going to be in the pure-food bill itself.

Senator LATIMER. In answer to your statement, I will say that I am a member of the Committee on Manufactures, and we have had hearings there on this subject for over two years.

Mr. YERINGTON. Yes; previously.

Senator LATIMER. Everybody that applied there has been allowed to be heard, after that bill was introduced in the Senate. You have admitted here that the provisions that you want in the bill were put in in the Senate, and then it went to the House, and after a full hearing there the House had inserted this item in committee and reported it to the Senate, where it went out on a point of order. That is the situation, as I understand it.

Mr. YERINGTON. On the agricultural bill.

Senator LATIMER. And the pure-food bill passed the Senate just as you say you would like to have it. Then it went to the House.

Mr. YERINGTON. There were other amendments that we were desirous of having at that time, Senator.

Senator LATIMER. But, I say, after a full hearing in the Agricultural Committee, the committee reported this amendment to the House, where it went out on a point of order. It is here now, and the pure-food bill is before the House; it was amended in the Senate as you asked and would like to have it, and is now being considered in the House. So that you have had a full hearing, it seems to me.

Mr. YERINGTON. I simply want to raise that point to show that the manufacturers did not intend by having that substitute introduced in the Senate to in any way retard the passage of the pure-food bill. That was not the object of having Senator Money introduce that as an amendment to Senate bill 88.   The Senate bill already having had consideration before your Committee on Manufactures and having been reported back favorably to the Senate, they saw that that was the only way they could have the bill printed and placed before the members of the Senate, hoping that from the discussion of the pure-food bill some points in our bill might be raised that would be acceptable to the provisions of the original Senate bill 88.   Now, you can see what has happened to the Senate bill.   As it came out of the Committee on Interstate and Foreign Commerce before the House, you will hardly recognize it as the Senate bill.

Senator LATIMER. Yes; but that was after full hearings.

Mr. YERINGTON. Oh, it was after full hearings.   Still, as Senator Heyburn said upon the floor of the Senate, his committee had had people before it for two or three years upon this bill that he introduced there and reported favorably; and at this time he did not think it necessary to go over that ground again for that reason.

Senator LATIMER. Yes.

Mr. YERINGTON. They had had those hearings and had gotten all the views of the manufacturers, and upon that they passed this bill in the Senate.   Now when it comes out of the House committee it comes out as a totally different bill.

Senator LATIMER. That is a question between the House and the Senate.

Mr. YERINGTON. Thoroughly so; but that was after all the manufacturers had had their hearing on this agricultural bill.

Senator LATIMER. There is one point I want to make with you: Not a member of this committee, as I remember, will be on that conference on the pure-food bill, so that we will have no dealings with it except in the Senate.

Mr. YERINGTON. I simply wanted to call attention to the fact that the manufacturers are perfectly willing to live up to all the provisions of that bill simply by having section 9 of it amended so as to require the Secretary of Agriculture to call upon this noninterested board of five chemists, and then that they, in collaboration with the others, should pass upon these questions as to the wholesomeness or unwholesomeness of these preservatives and any matter that may be added to food.   By that this association that I represent are willing to abide, and to live up to the requirements of the bill.   Of course they ask nothing that is unreasonable; they simply make it a little stronger in their behalf because they think that the board should be composed of disinterested experts, and they objected to that clause saying that that board was to be appointed solely by the Secretary of Agriculture prior to reaching any decision as provided for in this section.

It is not intended to speak disparagingly of the Department of Agriculture, of Secretary Wilson, and the others; but this provision gives such power that while in case Secretary Wilson's views should meet with the views of the manufacturers everything would go along very nicely, yet another Secretary of Agriculture might follow him whose views were diametrically opposed to those of Secretary Wilson; and this provision places unlimited power in the hands of that Department. By doing what the manufacturers request now you can provide for the appointment of this disinterested board to act in collaboration with the other two boards who shall pass upon these questions.

Senator LATIMER. On the other hand, if we fail to pass the pure-food bill we will have no legislation on the subject.

Mr. YERINGTON. You have your legislation to-day in all the various States, Senator, and this will not assist the manufacturers in the States at all, as far as the standards are concerned, because it does not empower them to create standards that they can be governed by in this appropriation bill. What the manufacturers want now is to have a pure-food bill pass Congress of such a nature that this question will be settled once and for all, and so that the various States in the Union can have their various laws amended so as to conform to the national law. I think that should be done, because the condition of things to-day is really very trying, as far as the manufacturing interests are concerned—that is, the laws are at variance in regard to labeling, etc. One thing is absolutely pure in one State that is absolutely a poison in the other, although they come out of the same kettle and are dipped by the same dipper from the receptacle into the vessels; simply the manner of labeling makes one pure in one State and a poison in the other. That is a condition that they are very desirous of having settled as soon as possible; and they are not here in any way to oppose the enactment of the pure-food bill, provided that they can be thoroughly protected, not only in the way of having an opportunity to have their day in court, but to be heard before a disinterested board in conjunction with somebody else.

The CHAIRMAN. The House bill as it came from the committee contained a provision that before any adverse publication was made notice should be given to the owner or manufacturer of the article, who should have a right to be heard, and on that testimony the matter should be decided. That provision was introduced.

Mr. YERINGTON. That was introduced; but in section 9——

The CHAIRMAN. The whole thing went out, of course.

Mr. YERINGTON. It went out. Now, one point that was raised that did not go out was that beginning on page 31, line 16, after the word "plants," in the appropriation bill. You will notice that the end of it went out, but they left that portion in; and that is fully covered by section 14 of the pure-food bill. That is on page 31, line 16, after the word "plants"—"And the Secretary of Agriculture, whenever he has reason to believe that any articles are being imported from foreign countries which are dangerous to health," etc.—that remains in there; but the clause that followed that went out. That provision is thoroughly covered in Senate bill 88, as reported from the House committee, in what is known as section 14. That entire clause was thoroughly covered by section 14.

Senator LATIMER. Why was that stricken out on page 32?

Mr. YERINGTON. It was intended that it should all go out on the point of order. You see it was covered in the act of August 30, 1890, chapter 839, "An act providing for an inspection of meats for exportation and prohibiting the importation of adulterated articles of food or drink and authorizing the President to make proclamation in certain cases, and for other purposes," together with the act approved July 24, 1897, to provide revenue for the Government "in regard to all articles of foreign manufacture, such as usually or ordinarily are marked, stamped, branded, or labeled under the tariff provision." That was all covered; and then section 14 of the bill thoroughly covered this provision here in regard to the powers of the Secretary of Agriculture as to articles of foreign importation, and the provision that I referred to of the act of August 30, 1890, thoroughly covers that matter as far as the Secretary of the Treasury is concerned.

The CHAIRMAN. I think we understand your position now.

Mr. YERINGTON. I have endeavored, Senator, to make that matter clear and also to endeavor to show the position of the Association of Manufacturers in regard to the passage of the pure-food bill. I assure you that they are very desirous of having it passed, but it is only natural that they should want to look out for their own interests. They thoroughly understood that with such a bill as passed the Senate they were to be protected; but, as I stated before, the Department to-day may take one view of this question, and under another Administration, if a change of Administration occurs, it may take another view of it. Under the provisions that they ask for in that amendment the entire matter is left with these boards to be appointed by the Secretary of Agriculture, whose action is to be for the information of the courts, and then they have their day in court. I think that will be perfectly satisfactory to the manufacturing interests, and, from what I am given to understand by them, they will endeavor to live up thoroughly to the provisions of the bill; and I think, once for all, that would settle that question.

I do not know that it is necessary to submit what I have here in writing. It simply covers the ground in regard to the two acts I have referred to—the act approved July 24, 1897, and the act of August 30, 1890.

The CHAIRMAN. We are glad to have heard your views, and we will look the matter over carefully.

(The committee thereupon went into executive session, after which it adjourned.)

INDEX.

O

B D 2.6.5

CPSIA information can be obtained
at www.ICGtesting.com
Printed in the USA
BVHW04s1030210918
528173BV00023B/1609/P